SECRETS TO REACHING
YOUR DESTINY

SECRETS TO REACHING YOUR DESTINY

HOW TO OVERCOME THE 7 MAJOR CHALLENGES IN LIFE

SALAY H. KEKULA

Library of Congress Control Number:		2011960436
ISBN:	Hardcover	978-1-4653-9537-5
	Softcover	978-1-4653-9536-8
	Ebook	978-1-4653-9537-5

All Scriptures quotations, unless otherwise indicated, are taken from the New King James. Copyright (C) 1982 by Thomas Nelson, Inc. Used by permission. All rights reserved.

Scripture quotations marked AMPLIFIED are taken from, The Amplified Bible, Old Testament copyright (c) 1965, 1987, by the Zondervan Corporation. The Amplified New Testament copyright (c) 1954, 1958, 1987 by The Lockman Foundation.

Scripture quotations marked MESSAGE are taken from THE MESSAGE. Copyright (C) by Eugene H. Peterson 1993, 1994, 1995, 1996, 2000, 2001, 2002. Used by permission of NavPress Publishing Group.

Scripture quotations marked NEW INTERNATIONAL VERSION or NIV are taken from the Holy Bible, New International Version, NIV (R), Copyright (c) 1973, 1978, 1984 by International Bible Society. All rights reserved.

Scripture quotations marked NLT or NEW LIVING TRANSLATION are taken from the Holy Bible, New Living Translation, copyright (c) 1996. Used by permission of Tyndale House Publishers, Inc, Wheaton, IL 60189 USA. All rights reserved.

Scripture quotations marked THE LIVING BIBLE or TLB are taken from The Living Bible copyright (c) 1971. All rights reserved.

To contact Author, go to www.secretstoreachingyourdestiny.com

This book was printed in the United States of America.

To order additional copies of this book, contact:
Xlibris Corporation
0-800-644-6988
www.XlibrisPublishing.co.uk
Orders@XlibrisPublishing.co.uk
302988

CONTENTS

Dedication

This book is dedicated to God the Father, the Son and the
Holy Spirit. I thank you Holy Spirit for being my teacher, guide
and greatest mentor. You promised to make all things possible
even though it might look impossible and you kept your
promise to me. Thank you!

ENDORSEMENTS

I thank God for this book, for it opened my eyes to the schemes of the enemy, prepared me to be victorious in battle and inspired me to be all that I can be in Christ Jesus. I am always encouraged when I speak to Salay, so I am very happy that he will be encouraging the millions who will read this powerful book. Salay, may God continue to impart into you his divine truths.

RHONDA DEVONISH (BA Hons)
Counselor

This book leads us to a wonderful scenario of human nature and uncannily accurate truth of self . . . I can say Its a spontaneous overflow of self experience and the biblical knowledge which energize and emphasize with exact examples . . . It shows and illustrates how to overcome the seven major challenges facing a significant person . . . Its absolutely a book of knowledge and power. God bless you Salay, for producing this great book.

SHERPHI HERIC ANTONIO
Managing Director
Orion London Ltd, Liverpool, UK

INTRODUCTION

You have a life purpose

You are a very significant individual created by God to accomplish a divine assignment. Have you ever asked the questions who am I and why am I here? These questions are as old as mankind and you are not alone in asking these old age questions. The truth of the matter is these are very two important questions to ask oneself. When you begin asking these questions, you have taken the initial step in discovering who you truly are.

One important thing you need to know is that there are challenges that are blocking you and attempting to blur your vision, and these obstacles are attempting to redefine you and put a label on you. They want to force you to doubt your identity and capabilities. It has been said by Dr. Myles Munroe that, "[1]The greatest weapon of the enemy is to produce feelings of self-doubt in an individual." The opposite of self-doubt is strong faith and believe in oneself. He did it to Adam and Eve (Genesis 3.5) and he is still attempting to do it to the rest of mankind (Matthew 4.3).

You have a potential

The obstacles seem to make you appear hopeless and aimless. Sometimes, they generate feelings that seem to be screaming 'you are not wanted or needed'. If you have ever felt that way, then you are reading the right book. This book is written for anyone who has experienced troubles that seems to hold you back from fulfilling your potential.

Why this book was written

It is written to console you and it is designed to equip you with power packed information. This information will reveal why negative things are happening in your life, how to put a stop to it and how you can take control back in every arena of your life and be in the driving seat of your destiny.

Root cause of the problem

Life is full of challenges and sometimes the feeling to give up on life and give in to despair and depression is constantly hunting lots of people.

Many people feel this way because society is not conducive to the personal development and cultivation of the seed and soil of your greatness. For instance, society will say to you, get a girlfriend or boyfriend but will not inform you of the responsibilities that come with it and what you need to know in order to manage and build a successful relationship.

In other words, society places demands on you but does not prepare you to meet those demands. No wonder there are many unhappy couples, and this also accounts for the reason the life span of the average marriage is diminutive.

Identify the source of the problem

However your real enemy is not society but it is an unseen alien creature that is referred to in the Bible as Satan, your enemy and the advesary of God. He is the one who sees you as a threat and as he has done through the ages, he comes to steal, kill and to destroy every good thing that concerns you when you give him access (John 10.10). He wants to come in the garden of your life and sow evil seeds of words that will eventually poison and disfigure the beautiful garden of your life.

Hold unto your dreams

He does not want you to rise above your present location in life. He wants to steal your dreams, and cause you to loose focus of your goals and objectives in life. He intends to eventually blind you from seeing the super star in you. Put simply, he intends to be in charge of the remote control of your life and stop you from pursuing your limitless possibilities.

As a significant person, you will face challenges because your enemy is constantly throwing doubts and unbeliefs at you. As a result, it is in your best interest that you are aware of the weapons that the enemy is using against you in order to steal your dreams, so that you can know how to handle and overcome those weapons effectively.

Your destiny is great

One thing you should never forget is that people who have great destinies are a threat to Satan; as a result he will do anything and everything to destroy their destinies. As a significant individual, by having knowledge of these challenges, you will be prepared to overcome them efficiently (Hosea 4.6).

Your vision will be fulfilled

The next reason this book was written is to help you identify these obstacles so that you can have an upper hand over the operation of the devil in your life and the lives of loved ones. In addition, by having knowledge of these challenges you will know what to do anytime the adversary is attempting to trap you. No matter the opposition to your purpose and destiny, you will be focused on achieving your vision as a result of the knowledge you will gain. The main reason the enemy bring these problems your way, is to break your focus.

Refuse to give up on your dreams

A broken focus gives an access point to Satan in your life and the consequence is unfulfilled potential. The devil wants to distract you from your purpose by presenting all sorts of wrong options and the devil may succeed if you allow him in through your ignorance, but the decision you made to read this unique book will result in a major turning point in your life.

The power in this book is like fresh air that will invigorate and energise you on your journey to reaching your destiny.

Understanding rejection

Understanding your past is only useful for understanding why you are the way you are right now. But once that's done, it's time to LOOK FORWARD to the FUTURE.

Marius

The stone which the builders rejected has become the chief corner stone. (Psalms 118.22, New American Standard Bible)

The first obstacle that is going to be discussed is rejection. What is rejection? Rejection is a negative action taken by one person against another person for various reasons. What could be the possible reasons a person may be rejected?

Those who have left you, don't deserve you

There are many possible reasons that may account for rejection. A person, institution or company may reject you because you have failed to meet certain requirements. A person may reject you because you refuse to behave like him or her. Rejection comes in diverse forms and one of the main sources of rejection comes from some friends, and even some family members.

Learn important lessons from every mistake

In the case of a significant person, as he or she keeps following their dream, they will lose some friends on the way who may not understand their path and reason for existence. There are some friends that you will be better off without because of their bad influence in your life. As you progress in life, you will not need friends who have no interest or desire for personal growth and development.

Be ready to make new friends

Your associations will have to change due to your destination. You will only need people in your social circle that will inspire you to aspire higher and achieve everything God has placed you on this planet to accomplish. Hence, understanding rejection is one of the ways God uses to keep you focused on the one most important thing in life and also to keep you on your destination.

Overcome the pain of rejection

When you are rejected by a friend, you may feel the pain of rejection but don't allow that to prevent you from moving forward. The pain of being rejected can be devastating for an individual who has a negative self-concept. When someone you did not expect to reject you rejects you, it generates many questions.

Rebound from rejection

The common questions you may ask are: what did I do wrong to deserve this kind of treatment? Is something wrong with the way I look or present myself? If those questions remain unanswered, the pain of rejection for instance by a fiancée may result in a broken spirit and this may result in depression. In extreme circumstances, unexpected rejection may lead to suicide attempts.

Reasons for rejection

God is going to remove certain friends from your life who are sent by Satan to hinder your progress. You don't need friends that are constantly bringing you down and discouraging you (Psalms 1.1-2). You should remember that whenever a person leaves your life, the reason is because God has someone better than the previous person who was in your life.

I want you to read that last sentence again and read it again until you get it.

Be careful about who you get close to

Consider analysing and categorising your friendships – such as those who are your permanent friends and those who are seasonal.

How would you know the distinction? By asking questions such as: Is this friend concerned about my progress or are they happy to watch me stumble? Is this friend reliable and dependable? Do they laugh at me or with me? Can I talk to them or do they do all the talking? When I'm in trouble do I feel safe sharing my weaknesses with them?

Learn to be emotionally independent

Be honest with yourself as you are your first best friend and this should help you to truly establish who your true friends are. When someone leaves your life, it may simply be that they were not fit to enter into your future. As with every life changing event, rejection by a friend should cause you to expand your personal network of friends and it should drive you to revaluate your life and make appropriate adjustments if necessary. The mistake most people make is that, the pain of being rejected causes them to close the door of their life from future possibilities of friends that God is preparing to release in their lives. Many take this action in order to prevent future rejection.

Understand the reasons for the seasons

There are many seasons in life and there are different types of friends that will come and go out of your life based on seasons. You may call the friends that are here to go as seasonal friends and those that are here to stay as permanent friends. There are friends God will allow in your life for a reason and for a season and as soon as their assignment in your life is completed, they depart from your life, some without warning and others with your consent. God will link you up with the right people who will serve as an advantage to your destiny.

God is protecting your life

When rejected by a friend, a relative or loved one that you did not expect to abandon you, do not think it is because something is wrong with you. The reason for rejection is for your protection, the betterment and preservation of your destiny, as there are some people that are a detriment to your progress and personal growth.

God, who knows all things, will remove that person who is a danger (as far as God is concerned) to your purpose and destiny.

Guard your divine destiny

The next reason for rejection is to keep your focus on what is most important in your life at this very moment. God is about to take you to a new place, a higher level in Him. Your friends are not willing to pay the price you are willing to pay. They will want you to remain with them and forfeit God's purpose and plan for your Life. God's plan and purpose is personal and you are responsible for taking control of your dreams and destiny. Where God is about to take you demands a great sacrifice. The sacrifice is worth the price because it will make you legitimate for the position and authority God has planned to entrust you with.

Keys to ovecoming rejection

Do not attempt to push any friendship because it will appear obvious that you are needy and desperate. The harder you attempt to seek a friend's approval the more likely he or she will begin to become more distant, and will not want anything to do with you. The main reason a friend may do this is because he or she sees you as a burden.

Seek God for your fulfilment

You have to grow to a point where you are self-validated, and you have to come to a place internally in your personal development where you are self-fulfilled. You must grow to a level where you do not need anything on the outside of you to make you feel good about yourself. When you come to a point where you are an independent individual, you look to God for your personal happiness and fulfilment and do not seek any approval from friends. Both external and internal barriers have to be overcomed in order for you to truely feel empowered on the deepest levels.

Internal power of self-actualized people

However it is going to take some discipline and committment to become self-actualized. When you are a self-actualized person, you decide your friendships and you decide the duration of those friendships. Put simply you control the fate of your personal relationships and how far you desire for them to last. You are the one with the power, the control; the influence and supreme confidence. You do have emotional power and fortitude against external forces and you do have the power to achieve anything you set your mind on to do. You are independent and do not have the need to cling to anyone. You are the one with the internal and external courage to organize and determine the outcome of your life.

God wants a relationship with you

Your relationship with God should be a primary priority in your life; it is possible for God to be so real to you that any other friendship becomes secondary. Have you ever heard the saying, "show me your friends and I will tell you who you are?" This saying is simple but it does sum up the necessity of choosing your friends carefully. My friend, God is available to you every moment and he desires to be the friend that sticks closer than a brother (Proverbs 18.24).

Three types of friends

Psalms 119.63 (Kings James version)

I am a companion of all who fear you, of those who keep your precepts

Qualities of first level friends

The first level friendships are those who are called by God to mentor you, no matter what stage you are in your life you will need some type of friends to ensure that you fulfil the call of God on your life and stay in line with what you are called to do.

They will support or dissuade you in the decisions that you may take because they are aware of the greatness locked up inside of you, even if they are unable to verbalise it. Their presence in your life will be of great value because they will enable you to get to your destination quickly and easily. Though they might not fully understand your purpose and vision, they will be there as your coach.

Essential qualities to cultivate

As a significant person, it is also imperative that, you have developed these essential qualities: you are a warrior within and you are prayerful. You are under the protection of a ministry. You must run after that ministry and you must renounce your past and you must serve the man of God in that ministry that God has led you to.

Always remember that, the Holy Spirit is your greatest mentor and you must get to know him on the deepest levels.

Identifying second level friends

The second level friends are those who you can share some of your secrets with and they will keep them confidential. These second level friends understand you better than most others, thus you can afford to be vulnerable before them (Matthew 26.37). They will defend you and may even offer to die with you (Matthew 26.35).

They have some idea about your vision. You will find that those most close to you are not many. However, you can rest assure that, in the midst of your trials, they will serve as an encouragement.

Detecting parasitic friends

Then there are the third level friends who are parasites. These are those who will follow you due to what you can do for them, not what they can do for you. I want to warn you concerning these kinds of friends because they are takers and not givers. You may call them parasitic friends. These friends can be identified through their selfishness and self-centredness. You must be careful in dealing with these groups of friends because they have an ulterior motive (Matthew 26. 14-16). In (Luke: 10.1), Jesus had seventy disciples but among those seventy, he had twelve who were close to him and amongst the twelve he had Peter, James and John who were even closer to him.

PRINCIPLE OF REJECTION

1 Samuel 17.28 (New International Version)

> When Eliab, David's oldest brother, heard him speaking with the men, he burned with anger at him and asked, "Why have you come down here? And with whom did you leave those few sheep in the desert? I know how conceited you are and how wicked your heart is; you came down only to watch the battle."

Never pay attention to critics

*T*he principle that governs rejection can be discerned in many stories in the Bible. The life of David shows an example of a young man who underwent a series of rejections. First, it started from some members of his family and the ruler of Israel. When the prophet Samuel came to anoint one of Jesse's sons as the next king, David was not considered by his father.

Although David was rejected by some members of his household he was ultimately recognised by God. One could say that, his rejection by King Saul led to David's promotion to the King of Israel. Other stories in the Bible like Jesus, Joseph exemplify the principle of rejection and the means by which the rejected become the selected.

Principle revealed

The principle that governs rejection can be stated as follows. **Anything that is rejected receives a divine recognition and divine recognition results in divine intervention and divine intervention ultimately leads to promotion and blessings.** Hence the principle of rejection states that rejection precedes promotion; it paves the way for your elevation.

When my Father and my mother forsake me, the Lord will lift me up (Psalms 27.16).

CRITICISM

"And ye shall be hated of all men for my name's sake" (Matthew. 10.22, King James version). "The disciple is not above his master, nor the servant above his lord. It is enough for the disciple that he is as his master, and the servant as his lord. If they have called the master of the house Beelzebub, how much more shall they call them of his household?" (Matt. 10.24, 25, King James version).

The next obstacle you will face as a significant person is criticism. The word criticism is defined by Collins dictionary and Thesaurus as "The act or an instance of making unfavorable or severe judgment; fault-finding."[1] The central phrase to note in that definition is 'fault-finding'.

Failure lifestyles of fault finders

As a significant person, you must be aware of the intention of Satan in criticizing you through a human being. The devil cannot communicate directly to you without a human being so beware of those who are doing nothing significant with their lives and are attempting to find fault with what God has called you to do. Most of these fault-finders have personal problems but instead of solving their problems, they pretend to have no problems and attempt to point out your problems.

---

[1]   Collins Dictionary and Thesaurus (UK: HarperCollins Publishers, 2000), 271

Negative people focus on your mistakes

This spirit will focus on what you do wrong and not what you do right. If you had the time to examine the life of those who are fault-finders, you would realize that they are frustrated chumps who are failures in their own right. They have nothing significant happening in their lives and so their idleness makes them available to point their finger on what someone else is doing with their life.

Destroy the assignment of a critical spirit

The spirit of criticism has an assignment from hell to stop you from doing what God has personally assigned you to do. As a significant person you must never forget the fact that what God has appointed you on this earth to accomplish will come under severe verbal attacks. The verbal attacks will come in the form of destructive criticism through the agents of Satan.

> When evildoers came upon me to devour my flesh,
> My adversaries and my enemies, they stumbled and fell.
> Though a host encamp against me,
> My heart will not fear;
> In spite of this I shall be confident.

(Psalms 27.2.3 King James Version)

Eliminate the negative seeds of criticism

Another assignment of the critical spirit is to sow seeds of doubt about self-concept and identity. Low self-esteem is a manifestation of the wound caused by a critical spirit. A spirit of criticism targets an individual in their time of weakness. It usually attacks an individual when they are vulnerable. When it strikes, an individual who experiences the pain will be wounded emotionally.

Effect of the critical spirit

The spirit of criticism has the ability and power to make you feel guilty and useless. A destructive critic majors on paralyzing its victim by making or portraying what they do as insignificant and a waste of time.

Rise above your critics and their words

A case in point is that of Nehemiah and the destructive critics whose sole motivation was to threaten and put an end to the project Nehemiah embanked on in Jerusalem.

"But it came to pass, that when Sanballat heard that we built the wall, he was wroth, and took great indignation, and mocked the Jews . . . Now Tobiah the Ammonite [was] by him, and he said, Even that which they build, if a fox go up, he shall even break down their stone wall" (Nehemiah 4.1, 4.3, King James Version)

Recognize invisible instructions in words

You should always remember the invisible instructions in words spoken to you either through a friend or an enemy. Every word spoken to you has an invisible assignment and command. When a destructive word is spoken, if not rejected, it will replay itself in your memory until you begin to believe what you heard. When you believe it, you have received it or you have given it a legal ground to perform its intended instructions in your life. It will eventually shape the way you view yourself and those around you. It will give you enough reasons to begin questioning certain areas of your life. The sign that you have received it is demonstrated through your "speaking". Spoken words are powerful!

Words are invisible seeds

The principle that governs words states that, every word that an individual hears and receives, that "word" will function to manifest the instructions in those words.

The story of Mary illustrates how powerful words can work to produce a desired result. The Angel Gabriel brought a word to Mary concerning the conception of Jesus and when Mary received the invisible seed, the word produced a result,

Words are potent

"And Mary said, "Behold the handmaid of the Lord; be it unto me according to thy word. And the angel departed from her" (Luke 1.38).

How did Mary receive the word of God? By hearing, believing and secondly she confessed it. She believed with her heart and confessed it with her mouth (Romans 10.9). In other words, she said to the Angel, I give a legal right for what you said to happen to me.

Words will always produce the desired results

The child Jesus was the result of Mary's acceptance of the word of God given by the Angel. Since the devil knows this principle also works in the negative realm, he uses it in the negative force of criticism to wound significant people, and those who give him access. You need to recognize the power of believing and make it work for you and not against you. When you hear and receive something you have align yourself with it but nothing happens until you speak. It is in your possession nevertheless and thus you are ready to activate your faith or fear. When you accept and begin speaking what you received, you have activated the instructions in those words to perform and manifest a desired outcome in your life. As soon as you confess or declare it, you have catapulted yourself in your believing. In other words, you have transported yourself in the reality of those words.

Disarm the pain of criticism

In the next paragraph the pain of criticism is the subject of our analysis. How the pain of criticism functions to affect an individual is central to our discussion. There is a pain that is generated by criticism that may lead to the one being criticised to fall into the trap of offence. The spirit of criticism can be seen as a weapon or medium used by Satan to inject offence. I will like to call offence a lethal injection.

Repsond positively to criticism

The success of Satan may be recognized based on how the individual who was criticized reacts or respond to the criticism. In order not to fall as the enemy intended, you need to understand how a fish responds to a worm when a fisherman throws it. The fish is unaware that in the worm is a hook that was designed to trap it and eventually kill it.

Be aware of this lethal injection

In the same way, you need to be aware that behind the criticism is a lethal injection (offence) that is intended to paralyze you and keep you on hold. You cannot progress in life as long as you hold unto offence and a grudge, and the devil is fully aware of that fact. You have to let go of offence from your heart, before you are subsequently released from that bitterness.

Forgive your offenders

Forgiving your offender is like vomiting a lethal poison from your system. As long as you carry that lethal poison (offence), you will be damaging your spiritual and emotional health and eventually your destiny.

Major Sources of Criticism

"And a man's foes shall be they of his own household" (Matthew 10.36)

The next source to look into is parental criticism and how a significant person overcomes a critical spirit if he or she is in good relationship with God.

If the source of criticism is from a mother or a father, one cannot determine the magnitude of the damaged caused because parents are a powerful force in their children's life either for good or for evil. Words spoken by Parents to children under any circumstance can be devastating, so can words spoken by people in authority over those beneath them.

Parents are influential

With regard to parents, if permitted, a critically destructive word can create more damage to a child's self-esteem and emotional development than can be outwardly observed. The influence of parents on their children's achievement or lack of achievement is critical. What parents say, whether it is to encourage or to criticize leaves an indelible mark on their children.

According to Jesus,

So every good tree bears good fruit, but the bad tree bears bad fruit.

(Matthew 7.17 King James Version)

Parents are the source of their children

Parents are the physical source by which their children are produced; hence children are the physical product of their parents. What Jesus was communicating is that, a person will be known according to their fruits. If you really desire to know how good a person is, find out from the fruit he or she is producing. The fruits that a person is bearing reflect that person and it speaks volumes about that person.

Children reflect their parents

As far as parents are concerned, outsiders should be able to notice the kind of parent you are just by looking at the behaviour of your children and their overall achievement in life. This is highly debatable because there are parents who are good natured and yet have children that are bad natured.

However generally speaking, how your children turn out as a person is mostly dependent on your level of involvement in their personal upbringing. In general, critical parents tend to raise critical children.

Children need lots of encouragement

Everyone has to take personal responsibility for themselves at a certain point in life, but young children living with their parents need lots of encouragement because the world only knows how to point out your weaknesses and what you do wrong. They are not a lot interested about what you do right.

Drop the fault finding attitude

If this kind of fault finding mentality is adopted by parents, it will lead to the raising of children who in many instances will act just like their parents. The finding fault mentality has to be obliterated since it does not solve a problem in your children but creates more problems. This is because that approach is the wrong one in bringing up young children. The truth is that approach should be dropped because it does not produce any good results.

Choose the right approach

The man or woman of significance is likely to raise children of significance because he or she only chooses the correct approach in raising his or her children. The significance person is likely to raise spiritual children who will reflect his or her character and way of life. Significant people will attempt to bring a balance between disciplining their children in the instructions of the Lord and at the same time, leaving room for children to take personal responsibility for their actions. In so doing, children grow up in an environment conducive for emotional, psychological and spiritual development which in turns prepares them for the outside world; it prepares them to be accountable and responsible.

Express your anger responsibly

The central reason parents criticize children is because of anger for something done wrongly. However there is a right way and a wrong way in achieving an intended objective. The manner by which parents express their anger can have a side effect on their child or children's development. What is anger? In this context, it is an expression that shows that you did not approve of the way your child has behaved. However there is a responsible way and an irresponsible way of expressing your anger.

Learn to deal wisely with a situation

The way a person expressess their anger is a sign of either their level of wisdom or lack of wisdom in dealing with a situation. As a parent, the way you choose to express how you feel about a child's behaviour will have a lasting impression on your child. In many instances, children will learn to express their anger as they saw their parent express theirs.

You are a role model

This is simply because, as a parent, one of your roles is a role model to your child. An action you perform in your role as a parent is being processed by your child who is constantly monitoring and learning from you. It is not a surprise to see that, perpetually angry parents have children who follow their footsteps. This actually begins with negative seeds of words sown in children on a daily basis.

Your actions speak louder

There is a saying that states, "Actions speak much louder than words". Your seed of actions and words toward your children will produce a harvest. If you do not like the current harvest, you need to change your approach and this begins with your awareness of God's word regarding children and also some awareness of child psychology.

Change your perception

As the beginning of change occurs through awareness, the following change will be observable as parents begin to see their children as God sees them. As far as

God is concerned, children are a heritage from Him and the fruit of the womb is his inheritance (Psalms 127.3). When parents come to an understanding that each child is significant, with a unique personality and with a God given gift and talent, their perception will change. As far as God is concerned, he has enthrusted you with his treasure or gift in a child He will hold you accountable for how you managed your child. You are only a caretaker of your child!

Nothing just happens

People of significance did not suddenly become a valuable asset to their generation without the quality investment from their parents. There is a saying I learned from Kenneth Copeland that goes like this: "Nothing just happens, everything or anything that ever happened can be traced back to a root cause."

Acquire knowledge and eliminate ignorance

Instead of sowing negative seeds of words of hostility, parents should change their misconceptions about children. This can be accomplished through the consultation of the wisdom of God concerning how to raise significant godly children.

As parents acquire and apply the knowledge they gained and with the help of prayer, children are likely to grow up to become significant men and women of positive influence in their generation.

Be aware of challenges

It is vitally imperative that, parents become aware of the various challenges associated with raising significant children in an ungodly society. Responsible and significant parents will not turn the responsibility of raising their children to the media, that is to say television or any other medium of communication. The social infrastructure is in moral decay; as a result it is not broadcasting the correct information to promote personal growth and fulfillment of destiny.

Society is disconnected from their source

The society preaches independence, not dependency on God. Since God is the source of parenthood you can trust his model and his principles and they will always work to bring about the intended result. No one ever followed the principles of God's word and was disappointed by the result. This is what God has to say about the power of his word:

> For as the rain and the snow come down from heaven,
> And do not return there without watering the earth

And making it bear and sprout,
And furnishing seed to the sower and bread to the eater;
So will My word be which goes forth from My mouth;
It will not return to Me empty,
Without accomplishing what I desire,
And without succeeding in the matter for which I sent it. (Isaiah 55.10-11
King James Version)

Overcome challenge presented by society

The problem of our society is it is in a serious mess because it is disconnected from God; hence, they lack the godly knowledge which only comes from God. Reliance on society and their various medium of communications will create more problems for parents and their children than can be solved, because they have disjointed value systems concerning principles for skillful living.

As a result of this awareness, parents will embark on the fruitful journey of taking personal responsibilty of raising their children in a godly manner.

Cultivate the leaders in your children

The price involved is temporary but the result is lasting and rewarding. Your children will be significant because they will be the leaders of tomorrow. They will, inturn, raise positive influential children to carry on the mantle of leadership to influence their generation to the glory of God. In every child is a leader waiting to be cultivated.

Seed of criticism produces dysfunctional personality

However if the seed of criticism is sown in a child from childhood, they may grow up with a dysfunctional personality. There are many young people growing up in broken homes and this issue can later become detrimental to them and to the society if they do not identify and deal with the root issue. The seed of poisonous words finds its roots or source in the poisonous force of criticism. Many at times, these criticisms come through emotional, verbal abuse and physical assaults.

Identify an agent of Criticism

An agent of criticism is a person who is hurting themselves and can't help but hurt others as a result. While words can be used as a building material for your life, the opposite is exactly the same. It can be used whether in ignorance or knowingly as a weapon of mass destruction.

Fault finders fosters your weakness

This spirit magnifies a person's short-comings with an intention to hurt and damage that person's reputation and self-esteem. A critical spirit can be seen to have its root in hatred and jealousy. If you are operating in love, you see everything from the angle of love. If you truly love a person, you would not want to see them damaged by your critical comments.

An agent suffers from self-hatred

Mostly, this could be rooted in self-hatred where a person is struggling with inferiority complex and does not appreciate who they are and hence they project this feeling on others they are in authority over.

Bitter people are the ugliest people

People who are miserable and bitter are the most mean and ugliest people around; as a result they feel they have a mission to make everyone else feel miserable. Their misery is recognized in their negative choice of words and negative attitude towards others. A person who hates themselves shows it in the way they treat other people closest to them.

Negative background of an agent

At times, it can be known that a critical individual is one who has highly developed the spirit of criticism. An agent is usually a person who does not know better than to criticize and tear people `down because while he or she was growing up, all they ever experienced was a critical atmosphere at home where the spirit of criticism ruled that home. A critical person can receive deliverance from the critical spirit if they have an intensive desire for healing past wounds in their lives (Proverbs 18.21).

Parental authority

Children obey your parents in the Lord, for this is right, "Honour your father and your mother" which is the first commandment with a promise: that it may be well with you and you may live long on earth. (Ephesians 6.1)

Special priviledge of being a parent

The entrusting of parental authority by God to parents placed them in a unique position over their children's future. The exercise of parental authority can have either a positive or negative effect. While parental authority can be used as a tool of blessing, it can also be used as an abusive tool.

Effect of parental authority

When used as a tool of blessing, it enhances, encourages, inspires, influences positively, and strengthens, but used negatively it disturbs the spirit and moral of a child. The negative results are low self-esteem, negative self-image, negative self-concept, self-hatred and self-abasement. The feelings of worthlessness, insecurity, negative mindset, negative outlook, and inferiority complex in a child are all consequences of parental criticism and neglect.

Don't abuse your authority

One of the ways parent may exercise this unique gift to produce the maximum benefit in children is using their words to bless their children on a regular basis. When parents discover that secret, they can influence their children's life positively through the exercise of words of blessings. It will dawn on them that they have an awesome role in determining the outcome of their children's future to some extent.

Use your words as a channel of blessing

Parents should realise that they can use their words to release their children in doing great exploits in the kingdom of God, and to empower children for life's many opportunities and limitless possibilities. However, the abuse of this unique gift by some parents is due to gross ignorance and misconceptions adopted or passed on from one generation of parents to the next. Nevertheless you could be the first person to change all that because you are a new creation.

Behold, if any man be in Christ, he is a new creation, old things have passed away and behold all things have become new (2 Corinthians 5.17 King James Version).

Don't misuse spiritual Law of words

When parents release words in their mouth, either a word of blessing or cursing, they have activated the spiritual law of words. Jesus said, "The words that I speak to you are spirit and they are life." Put simply, words are efficient, words are not empty, and they are full of divine efficacy. There is a law that governs words and when this law is activated, it functions to execute the assignment or invisible instructions in those words.

It is the Spirit who gives life; the flesh profits nothing; the words that I have spoken to you are spirit and are life (John 6.63).

Consequences of misuse of the law of words

Lack of knowledge and misuse of this law of words by some parents is the cause of many young people's behaviour problems. Most of these children who are victims are marked by perpetual lack of direction, lack of a sense of purpose, and lack of motivation for life, which eventually lead to an unproductive and irresponsible lifestyle.

Parent should educate themselves

On the contrary, when parents identify that they are the source of most of their children's behaviour problems, they can make a positive difference. When they realise the enemy through their ignorance is using them to interfere in their children's future through the law of words, they will be awoken to the reality and authority that parenthood carries.

Parents can conquer misconceptions of parenthood

As parents rise up to conquer the spirit of ignorance concerning parenthood and that is to say the lies of society concerning raising children, they will begin to see positive differences in their children's mindset and behaviour.

Parents should thirst for God's word

Parents will achieve this through a deliberate thirst and acquisition of godly knowledge. When parents educate themselves with godly truths regarding raising children, then they are in a better position to educate and train their children who will rise to influence their generation for God's kingdom (Proverbs 22.6).

Death and life are in the power of the tongue, and those who love it will eat its fruit. (Proverbs 18:21)

Negative side effects on children

The lack of parental guidance in the day to day up bringing of children is the main source of many children's problems. The difference is seen between children brought up in an environment that specialised in criticising and those who grew up in a home that specialised in giving love and encouragement. One of the side effects on children is their inability to successfully develop fruitful relationships with others.

Words can destroy relationships

This is because one important key to building a healthy relationship with other people is your choice of "words". Words are what are responsible for building great relationships and they are also responsible for destroying relationships.

Words are responsible for making us or unmaking us, thus one must be conscious of what to say, and say it in the right tone of voice and at the right time. For the way you choose to say something can determine the outcome of any communication either negatively or positively.

Develop interpersonal skills in your children

That is why it is important that parents invest time developing social skills and other important interpersonal skills in order to give children an upper hand and edge in life instead of constantly criticising them.

Relationships flourish in a positive atmosphere

A good and a productive relationship cannot flourish in an environment that promotes fear, belittlement and threats, and treats other people as though they don't deserve to be treated as a single, valuable and precious individual, created by God in a unique way to fulfill a purpose in God's over all plan for humanity.

Critical spirit produces insecurity

The next side-effect on a child growing up in a critical home is the feeling of insecurity. The child feels insecure because a critical spirit creates a stronghold of fear; this is the worst stronghold to have since it paralyzes you. In fact, fear is the one major devastating result caused by a critical spirit at home. A child growing up in a home where the only thing that is pointed out is his or her faults and weakness may create insecurity in that child. The spirit of criticism has the tendency to only want to point out a person's mistakes.

Parental assignment

The role parents play in bringing up a significant child in a ruthless and merciless environment is especially crucial in this generation. As parents discover how they can contribute extensively in training and shaping their children's future or giving them a good start in life, they will commit to that noble course of raisng significant children.

Parents are custodians

A significant person did not suddenly become a world changer, it took the valuable contribution of various people but the role of parents is absolutely paramount. More importantly, the values thought and lessons learned at home while a child was raised, became crucial to further self-actualization of a child of significance.

A significant child refuses to be a victim

In some cases, a child who grew up in an abusive home can later grow up to become a significant individual who is making a difference in the life of other people who suffered from destructive criticism as well.

God will use you mightily

Usually, that is only made possible through God who takes such an individual and transform them from having a victim mentality to a victor mentality. It is amazing how God can take hold of an individual and completely transform their mindset, build their self-esteem and make their life a success story (Acts 13.22).

Critical spirit targets self-confidence

The ultimate intention of this spirit is to cause damage to a person because they are unable to defend themslelves against the attacks. It also attacks in order to destroy self-confidence so as to render its victims hopeless and powerless. The use of mother or father figures by the spirit of criticism is usually the devil's favourite agent in fulfilling his assignment of destruction.

Always remember that, the assignment of Satan is to destroy whatever good thing you have and your children could not be an exception.

Put on your armour of war

Wherefore take unto you the whole armour of God that ye may be able to withstand in the evil day, and having done all, to stand. Stand therefore, having your loins girt about with truth, and having on the breastplate of righteousness; And your feet shod with the preparation of the gospel of peace; Above all, taking the shield of faith, wherewith ye shall be able to quench all the fiery darts of the wicked. (Ephesians 6.13-16)

Overcome Criticism from society

The next major source of criticism is the society. This is the challenge of a life time in the lives of significant people. Due to his or her responsibilities a person of significance is constantly engaged with society.

They do have supporters in the community and in society as a whole but not everyone appreciates the changes they are causing due to the gifts and the anointing of God upon their life. There is a saying which states that, "greatness attracts trouble". But greatness also attracts admirers as well.

Significant person has challenges to overcome

While the person of significance will attract admirers, he or she will also attract satanic agents whose intentions are to bring him or her down. The spirit of criticism at this level operates at a higher degree because the society especially those who do not understand the significant people assignment will attack them.

You have a superior spirit

There is a saying that goes as follows: "Every new level attracts new devils." However, every new level also attracts higher level of angels in your life for the purpose of assisting you.

You will not keep dealing with the same devils because the higher your rank in the spirit, you begin dealing with higher levels of principalities. You can rest assured that, you are a higher and a super principality because you are sitting with Christ in the heavenly places.

And hath raised us up with Him, and seated us with Him in the heavenly places in Christ Jesus, (Ephesians 2.6)

Necessity of criticism

The significant person must know that, the obstacles faced while living at home were all part of the process of growing and character development of which most great men and women of God experience. If you are experiencing some of these major challenges we are learning about now, you must count yourself previledged because you could have been chosen for a special assignment. You are being trained for your special assignment!

Criticism paves the way for promotion

The criticism experienced while at home was necessary because it was to make the significant person ready for the subsequent trials needed for the next level in the spirit. The challenge of criticism is one of the most painful and yet useful test for promotion.

You cannot be promoted without first passing the test of criticism and you must embrace the opportunity to be criticised if you desire to be used by God. While the enemy meant it for evil, God turns it around for your good.

Be aware of agents of darkness

The more you come to the limelight, the more you become dangerous to the devil because God will start to use you to plunder his kingdom. This will cause reaction in the devil's kingdom.

Satan will begin to use his human agents to talk evil about you. You must never forget that, every progress you make will generate anger in Satan's kingdom because your growth means more power is being handed down to you by God to plunder the devil's kingdom.

Ignore the books written to redicule you

This might include books written to insult you and try to destroy your reputation in order to stop your influence. They will lie on you and talk evil about you. Taking some of what you have said out of context to make you appear as though you were a deceiver. One of the reasons for this severe criticism and persecution is to cause you to lose focus.

Recognise Distraction

Let me dwell on this issue of distraction. Distraction is one of the sole reasons for all this criticism levelled at you by the public or the media. They want to distract you so that you lose focus on what is most important to you. What God has called you to accomplish is your focus in life and not what others are saying or doing.

The enemy is highly interested in your position

Everyone has a calling, while some have perverted theirs; it causes them to become idle and busy bodies in other people's businesses. In order to keep your focus, you must ignore some of these critics.

Satan who was once Lucifier, lost his position as the anointed cherub and we are all seeing the consequences (Isaiah 14.12-15). Since a loss of position results in purposeless existence, it is critical that you hold unto your position because the devil wants your position.

He distracts you to steal your position

The devil from experience has known that, distraction is one of the effective ways he removes significant people from their position of authority and he is still using this strategy because it has always worked for him. It worked for him in the Garden of Eden when he deceived Adam and Eve.

The devil is an authority stealer

The whole temptation was about identity. God said Adam and Eve were like him. But the Devil came and said they were not like God until they ate the fruit. You see how the devil operates; he always tries to make you believe that God is a liar.
God is not a man, that He should lie,
Nor a son of man, that He should repent;
Has He said, and will He not do it?
Or has He spoken, and will He not make it good? (Numbers 23.19 King James Version)

Recognize unhealthy attractions

There are so many attractions and distractions hunting the significant person. Most of these are unhealthy and are designed by the devil to break the focus of the significant person who is constantly exposing his activities, and when you keep exposing Satan he will not sit back, he will attack and those he uses are demonic and satanic personalities.

The enemy is jealous of your exalted position

Not everyone who laughs with you likes you. Somebody may be laughing with you and yet plotting your downfall. Watch out for false pretenders who appear honest on the outside but deep within, they could be filled with jealousy and hatred.

The devil has human agents

Remember, Satan is the god of this world. Most of the rulers if not under the leadership of the Holy Spirit are controlled by Satan. Does Satan have agents at every human institution? Yes he does! The devil has human agents every where who may appear good but they work for Satan whether they are conscious of it or not.

Guard the anointing

Keep your eyes wide open and keep yourself in daily prayer because it produces daily anointing for overcoming the daily strategies of the devil. With the discernment of the Holy Spirit which comes through the anointing, and by the gifts of the Holy Spirit you will know such persons. A sign to watch out for is a person who has a habit of releasing curse words. When you notice that sign, you can be sure that, that individual is under the influence of an evil spirit and they need deliverance.

The anointing is precious

There is something you have got that the devil wants to steal from you. Remember that he is a thief and he is always looking for an opportunity to steal from you (John 10.10). So make sure that you give him no access or an opportunity through sin and make sure you have on the whole armoured of God.

The anointing is a weapon of mass destruction

The anointing you have got on your life is what the devil is after. He knows the absolute necessity of the anointing because since he corrupted his, he is deprived of authority and the power to function as God originally intended, as a result he is malfunctioning.

Be aware of your enemy strategy and intent

He knows if he can deceive you to get you to poison your anointing, you will also lose your position and power to function as God intended. If he can succeed in deceiving you to poison and corrupt your anointing through sin, then he knows that you have ceased to be a threat to his kingdom.

Don't negotiate your position

The devil goes after those that are a match and a threat to his kingdom. What you need to know about the anointing is that, it makes you stand out. It is the anointing that enables you to destroy the works of the enemy and so, without it, you are vulnerable and you actually become useless to God.

The anointing attracts jealous people

The anointing makes negative people jealous; it brings satanic agents around you. The anointing on your life will make people appear to like you but deep within their hearts, they despise you and are planning to bring you down.

Protect your most precious commodity

You cannot underestimate the importance of the anointing upon your life. The reason a significant person is recognized as such is because of the anointing upon their lives. Without it, you become insignificant. The anointing is the power of God and it can be lost, so fight to maintain and keep it. It is a precious substance and it can easily be lost.

But you have an anointing from the Holy One, and you all know (1 John 2.20)

You are wiser than your adversary

When you know that behind these attacks by the public, there are wicked spirits assigned by hell to distract you, it should put you on guard, ready at all times to defend your ministry through fellowshipping with God. Since we are not wrestling against flesh and blood but against spirits, you must be prayerful.

For we wrestle not against flesh and blood, but against principalities, against powers, against the rulers of the darkness of this world, against spiritual wickedness in high places. (Ephesians 6.12 King James Version).

Prayer sustains and preserves the anointing

It is prayer that sustains the anointing upon your life. Prayer is a major key that will keep your ministry advancing. Fellowshipping wth the Holy Spirit and deepening your relationship with him are the ways you become alert to the activities of the enemy. The enemy uses human beings knowingly or unknowingly to carry out the plans of Satan.

Speaking in tongues activates the power of God

So we have to be on alert for little devils that are sent from the pit of hell to distract us. Watch out for the little foxes that come to destroy the vine.

Catch us the foxes, the little foxes that spoil the vines, for our vines have tender grapes (Songs of Solomon 2.15)

The god of this World

The next reason for the attack by some people in the public is connected to the god of this world. The devil manifests himself in different forms and there are different names to identify exactly what he is doing in the lives of those who are under his dominion at particular time and location.

The devil is inferior and void of power

You must understand that, the god of this world is the controller of the affairs of men and when I say men, I am talking about those who are not born again. Due to this, you need to identify your real enemy if you are to put things in proper perspective.

The enemy lives in an unseen realm

When you realise that your real enemy is not your sister, brother, mother or father you will know how to handle persecutions and criticism more wisely.

Jesus said,

> "Behold, I send you out as sheep in the midst of wolves. Therefore be wise
> as serpents and harmless as doves" (Matthew 10.16).

Since you became part of the kingdom of the Lord Jesus Christ, you became a target to Satan and his cohorts. This is why as a significant person; you have to be aware of the two spiritual kingdoms we exist in.

Pray and don't faint

The moment you stop praying, the moment you stop operating in the daily anointing that is released upon you each time you go before God in prayer and the moment you stop studying the scriptures, you have open yourself up for an attack.

Walk and function in God's wisdom

The way the devil operates is very subtle and sophisticated and that is why you need to understand the realm of the spirit. The operation of the enemy is revealed in the scriptures to those who walk and practice the word of the Lord.

The righteousness of the blameless makes his path straight but thorns and snares await those who follow crooked paths (Proverbs 11.5).

You must constantly live a life from a spiritual standpoint if you are to remain successful and productive in the Lord Jesus Christ, the image of the invisible God.

In whose case the god of this world has blinded the minds of the unbelieving so that they might not see the light of the gospel of the glory of Christ, who is the image of God. (2 Corinthians 4.4)

Accept Correction

Instead of allowing criticism from the religious people or society to distract you, you should consider the criticism to examine any area you are going wrong and correct yourself immediately.

Paul was accused of insulting the high priest and he responded by pleading and accepting responsibility for his actions (Acts 23.4). However, if it happens to be false accusations, as a significant person you have to stand your ground in the physical as well as in the spiritual realm.

Be aware of spirits assigned to bring you down

There are spirits that are specifically targeted at a person of significance and their sole intent is to hinder and stop you from pursuing your vision. Some of these spirits specialise in finding faults and magnifying it through the critical spirit. These spirits keep record of little faults that they see you make.

Refuse to fall for the traps

In order to not fall in the trap set by these spirits which creates an opportunity to find faults, a significant individual must be prayerful. You must be on your guard at all times in prayer. You must remain an intercessor for the kingdom of God. You must guard the presence of God against the pollution of the enemy. You must avoid the negative people around you. You must fight the good fight of faith.

Fight the good fight of faith; take hold of the eternal life to which you were called, and you made the good confession in the presence of many witnesses (1 Timothy 6.12).

Keys to healing the wounds of criticism

The Spirit of the Lord is upon me, because he hath anointed me to preach the gospel to the poor; he hath sent me to heal the broken-hearted, to preach deliverance to the captives, and recovering of sight to the blind, to set at liberty them that are bruised, and to preach the acceptable year of the Lord (Luke 4.18)

You have a triumphant spirit

A person of significance is not necessarily an individual who happened to have had parents who were educated on the concept of parenthood. A significant person is a man or a woman who turns his losses into gains. This individual trades his abuses into victories by the anointing of the Lord.

Cultivate a winning attitude

He or she changes his victim mentality into a victor and a more than a conquerer mentality through the word of God. Emotional damage is traded for a stable emotional state and also into an emotion that is completely strong, secure, healthy and ready to teach others how they too can heal their damaged emotions through listening to God's prescription for divine health.

Receive Emotional healing

It is true that, a person of significance is a person who may have been once a victim damaged by criticism but through Jesus Christ, he or she received healing and restoration. Jesus does understand the pain because he was once a victim of criticism and physical and emotional abuse (Isaiah 53.5).

Joel 2.22

> And I will restore to you the years that the locust hath eaten, the cankerworm, and the caterpillar, and the palmerworm, my great army which I sent among you.

The Presence of Jesus is a healing presence

That is why victims of destructive criticism who take their wounds to Jesus through fellowshiping with him on a daily basis will begin to experience healing in their lives through the presence of Jesus.

A person of significance is most of the time a person who is able to overcome the seven major challenges, to become a testimony to those who have been through similar circumstances but felt like, they could not overcome it.

Receive your healing in God's presence

The only solution for healing the wounds is the presence of the Lord. The presence of Jesus is a healing presence because it brings total restoration. The presence of God is the place of receiving new strength and anointing to overcome (Isaiah 40.31). The presence of God brings refreshment from above.

Jeremiah 30.17 (New International Version)

But I will restore you to health and heal your wounds,' declares the LORD, 'because you are called an outcast, Zion for whom no one cares.'

DESTRUCTIVE CRITICISM

There are essentially two types of criticism, namely, constructive and destructive criticism. Destructive criticism usually comes from a person who hates you and they display this hatred by "insulting" you and sowing doubts about your calling and reason for existence on every available voice.

A destructive criticism as it is rightly called results in injury of the person being criticised. It is sent to belittle, to demoralize and to sow seeds of fear and to cause an individual to feel negative about their live.

Don't focus on the criticism

However, this kind of criticism should not be allowed to perpetuate due to its damaging nature.

Spending time in the presence of God will make a person who has been a victim of that kind of emotional abuse to receive complete healing. A victim of destructive criticism should also pray for the person who is causing or has caused injury in their life because this is all part of the healing process.

Pray and intercede for your critics

When you go before Jesus regarding any criticism, the first thing he will ask you to do is keep praying for the person who is doing it to you. Don't be like them bless them if they are cursing you, and also exercise walking in love on purpose. Bless them and pray for God's healing and forgiveness in that person's life.

You don't have to associate with them but make sure you do not fall for the trap and intention of Satan by participating in their wrong behaviour. Always overcome evil with good.

Do not be overcome by evil, but overcome evil with good. (Romans 12.21)

Crucial points to remember about your critics

A destructive criticism is designed and sent by Satan through a human vessel in order to destroy a person's self-esteem. A destructive critic only point out your faults and tiniest mistakes. These critics are always looking for any opportunity to tear down their victims whether they know they are under Satan's influence or not.

Respond in love

Some of these criticisms are manifested through the lies that are told about you through fault findings. Destructive critics do not love you and do not care about your well being. The hatred in them towards you will manifest through "words of hostility." What they are really after is your reaction and you should always respond in love.

Don't participate in their wrong behaviour

They want to see you completely silenced, ineffective and feeling sorry for yourself. In order not to partake of their evil deeds, you must keep yourself away from their presence. They are the negative people around you and you must avoid them like the plague. These group are distractors and dream killers.

Your critics are blinded by Satan

Unknowingly, they are blinded and walking in the darkness of ignorance and misery. In order not to be contaminated by their evil words, remember that when you choose to respond, it should be done only when you have prayed, thus you will respond in love and avoid strife and guard yourself against strife. Strife will open a door to Satan in your life and where strife is, God's presence is not.

Handle persecution wisely

This is all part of the persecution Jesus talked about for the reason of the anointing. Jesus said to his disciples,

> "Blessed are ye when men shall persecute you and insult you for my sake, rejoice and be exceedingly glad, for great is your reward in heaven. For so persecuted they the prophets who were before you" (Matthew 5.11)

Your critics have no purpose in life

As I said earlier on, they might write books concerning you or articles to talk bad about you or even frame you to accuse you falsely on youtube or any other social media. However, you must maintain your ground in prayer by seeking God at all times.

Your critics hate your difference and uniqueness

As long as we are in the world, there are critics out there who will oppose the work of God and say all sorts of nasty things about it. Most of these critics are in the body of Christ who claim to have a calling to criticise.

Display of hatred is by criticism

Jesus said we are in the world but we are not of the world and because we are not of the world, the world hates us and they demonstrate this hatred through criticism. They are just wasting their time because Jesus will build his Church and the gates of hell shall not prevail against it.

Let your success be apparent to all

Keep persevering and keep focus on your call. You as a significant person must keep growing in faith and love so much so that, your success in the things of God will be evident by both your critics and your fans.

Take pains with these things; be absorbed in them, so that your progress will be evident to all (1 Timothy 4.15).

CONSTRUCTIVE CRITICISM

For whom the LORD loveth he correcteth; even as a father the son in whom he delighteth. (Proverbs 3.12 King James Version)

Those who love you will always correct you

Constructive or positive criticism is spoken out of love and is spoken by people who care for you deeply and are interested in your welfare and your progress. They bring correction and improvement to what you do. The Bible says, a wise man accepts correction but a scoffer rejects it and suffers the consequences (Proverbs 15.12).

Correction required for your personal development

Accepting correction is necessary for your continual growth and development. It even pays to do self-analysis and ask for other people's opinion and evaluation of what you do but only by those that love you so that you can keep getting good and better at what you do until you become very great. Positive criticism or constructive feedback gives you a different and probably a better perspective of yourself and what you do for God.

Do self-analysis regularly

It helps you to identify where you are at in your personal development and it also helps to point out your weaknesses so that you can work to eliminate them for good. A significant person is always looking for opportunities for personal improvement because he or she seeks excellence. Humility then can be said to be one of the signs in identifying a significant person (James 4.10).

Chapter summary

In the last chapter, we examined the seed of criticism and how the enemy tries to sow it in the life of a significant person in order to stop them from fulfilling their destiny. We have observed that a critical spirit is not of God. Anything that is not of God has to be resisted at all cost. The best way to deal with the spirit of criticism is through prayer and responding to the criticism in the love of God. Have you ever heard the saying, 'Love conquers all'?

"Love never fails" (1 Corinthians 13.8).

Satan is your invisible enemy

You noticed that, we identified the source of criticism as Satan (an invisible enemy). We identified Satan as the source of destructive criticism and he uses human beings and these vessels are living in ignorance of God's word. Hence you should be addressing Satan to leave those vessels instead of trying to fight a losing battle by attacking those vessels. When the devil is dealt with, his attempts to destroy becomes disabled (James 4.7).

Discern a critical spirit

Every time a critical spirit is present or is operating, you must guard your heart against contamination through fellowshipping with the Holy Spirit and those who walk with him. A critical spirit tends to manifest in different forms based on the situation. At one time, it is a lying spirit and the father of lies is Satan.

Use your faith filled words to tame Satan and his system

1 John 5.4 for everyone born of God overcomes the world. This is the victory that has overcome the world, even our faith.

Deal with issues as they arise

So the only way you can overcome is deal with Satan in the spirit realm through your faith filled words and declarations. You must understand the realm of the spirit before overcoming the battle over destructive criticism. After that, expect him to flee from your presence. When you resist him steadfastly, he will have no choice but to flee swiftly.

Submit therefore to God Resist the devil and he will flee from you. (James 4.7)

ISOLATION

Then Jacob was left alone; and a Man wrestled with him until the breaking of day. (Genesis 32.24)

*W*hat is isolation? According to the Concise Oxford Dictionary, Isolation is "The act or instant of isolating; the state or quality of being isolated or separated."[2] Isolation is not necessarily an absence of people but it is a season that most significant people experience.

Embrace your season of grooming

It is a time of cultivation and grooming and it is also a season of lack of recognition by others. Moreover it is a season of preparation, separation unto God for training for reigning. No one even notices you or acknowledges your existence. Why? Because you are still a seed and you are still under the soil (1 Peter 1.23).

You are under preparation and training

People are still walking all over you and sometimes you feel hopeless and frustrated. Joseph is a typical example of one who was isolated from his family for a reason and for a season (Genesis 37).

---

[2]   The Concises Oxford Dictionary (Oxford: Clarendon Press, 1995), 722

David is another typical example of one who experienced isolation and God took that period to prepare and train him for the greatest experience of his life. Moses was another significant person who had a great destiny but needed to be separated for preparation and training purposes (Exodus 2.11-25).

Jesus is another typical example of one who was led in the wilderness and separated for a period for a reason and for a season (Matthew 4.1).

You are special and selected by God

Can you already observe a major trend? You can see that those who experience a season of isolation and separation are those with great destinies. If you are experiencing isolation now at this very moment, you should be comforted because you could be a great man or woman of destiny and you are among the company of great and extremely rare people.

Understanding isolation

There is a season of Isolation and it is a time of getting to know God better. Most people spend the majority of their whole eixstence getting to know people but the significant person does the exact opposite. The significant person knows that, he came out of God, meaning his origin is of God and he came on this planet not as a result of an accident or coincedence but by God's ordained plan and predetermined purposes (Ephesians 1.8-12).

Significant people have strong sense of purpose

He or she knows that, in order to fulfill his or her destiny, knowing God personally is a vital priority to finding meaning and fulfillment in this life. The significant person knows that, there are different levels to getting to know God and your public ministry to the world is dependent on your private relationship with God and there are different levels to it. That is why understanding the reason and season of Isolation is very crucial.

Importance of Isolation

The season of isolation is important because it offers an opportunity in the life of a significant person to develop a deeper relationship with God and thereby developing character (Character is your foundation). So many people have a shallow relationship with God and this keeps them ineffective for God and the outside world. A time of isolation is a moment of aloneness with almighty God for transformation and impartation. God will isolate you in order to protect you from the plans of the enemy.

You are in a season of empowerment

A time of isolation is a period of being endued with power from on high (Acts 1.8). God takes personal responsibility for your life because he has a plan for your life and he isolates you to prepare you for the task he has planned for your life before you were born (Jeremiah 1.5).

Gain a solid foundation

One of the reasons of isolation is to develop durability, stability and longevity in a significant person's life.

Durability means, "To be able to perform or compete over long period as by avoiding or overcoming injuries." The word stability means, "Resistant to change of position or condition; not easily moved or disturbed." Longevity means, "long life or great duration of life." One important principle of life is that, anything that is untested cannot last.

Challenges are stepping stones to your greatness

Testing determines quality and quality determines longevity. Every relationship will come into a season of testing. God may remove some people out of the way in order to do the work he purpose to do in your life. As long as those people are in your life, they serve as a distraction and hindrance to your advancement.

Avoid the negative people in your life

The negative people's presence in your life are not conducive for what God intends to do in your life. Understanding this most important principle of isolation will help you to stay focus even in the midst of rejection. A time of isolation is a major challenge because if not understood, you may feel like; life has no purpose whatsoever and you may feel like the whole world is against you. Some friends may have left you right now and it may be the will of God.

God cares for you deeply

God does not want you polluted by negative people and if he allows that person in your life, they may pollute you and damage your divine destiny. God is very interested in every detail of your life and he wants you fulfilled and happy so he will watch over you and make sure no one messes with you if you allow him. God ultimately has the best for you and that is exactly what he is preparing you to get.

Day by day the LORD takes care of the innocent, and they will receive an inheritance that lasts forever.

They will not be disgraced in hard times; even in famine they will have more than enough (Psalms 37.18.19, The New Living Translation)

An appointment with God

A time of isolation demands that you are left alone for the purpose of God meeting you to change you and transform you into the image of Christ. Only those who are truly transformed can make a positive difference in this world. When you are yielded to the Holy Spirit training his ultimate intention is to empty the world out of you. It is also a time where God wants to strip Egypt out of you so that he can fill you with all wisdom and spiritual understanding. Before Moses was allowed to go back to Egypt, God made sure that Moses was completely empty of Egypt during his wilderness experience.

Be transformed by the renewing of your mind

You should note that Egypt is symbolic of the world system. Before you bring change in this troubled and confused world as a significant person, you need to have experienced a transformation in your life first and foremost. You can only give what you have and lots of people are trying to give something they don't have.

Experience complete freedom before you free others

Lots of people are trying to free someone from something that they themselves are struggling with. What a pathetic situation! You must always remember that, a change in you qualifies you to bring change in the life of others.

Grow in grace and knowledge

One of the signs of identifying a significant person is that they have overcome the seven major challenges, and were able to conquer them through the knowledge of God. As a result of their solid relationship with God, they began to experience changes in their lives as they cultivated a kingdom mentality. They developed a greater confidence in God's ability as they became aware of the realities of his kingdom.

2 Peter 3.17

"Therefore, dear friends, since you already know this, be on your guard so that you may not be carried away by the error of lawless men and fall from your secure position. But grow in the grace and knowledge of our Lord and Savior Jesus Christ. To him be glory both now and forever! Amen," (New International version).

Learn a lesson from Moses mistake

Moses was convinced that, he was doing the work of God when he killed an Egyptian (Exodus 2.14). Moses ran for his life to live in Midian (Exodus 2.15). As time unfolded, God worked with Moses and made him into a great leader. From God's divine plan, Moses was destined for greatness. However, God also knew that, Moses was not ready and secondly, his location made it difficult for God to begin the process of training and purification.

You know your divine assignment

Moses was also aware of his purpose but did not know exactly how and when to carry it out. Day in and day out, Moses would see his Hebrew brothers and sisters suffering but could not do anything about it. One day however, he decided to take matters into his own hands and got in trouble. As a result he had to run for his life.

Pursue a personal encounter with God

How many people in our generation are exactly like Moses who has a passion to bring a change in other people's life but are doing it the wrong way because they have not had a personal encounter with God? This is a crucial question for those wishing to go into ministry. How prepared are you for the call of God on your life? Has God anointed you and shown you exactly how to carry out the ministry he called you into? How would you describe your encounter with God that marked your inauguration into the ministry? The call of Moses should teach you a lot about the importance of making sure that, you have been called to do whatever you want to do for God. (Exodus 3.10)

Work to become "the called of God"

Moses was called to do something great but Moses was not yet "The called", when he took matters into his hand. In order to be "The called" of God, you must be wholly yielded to the leading of the Holy Ghost and he will speak to you about how to go about the work He has called you to accomplish. (Romans 8.27, Rm 8.16)

Right location

Location is also a major fundamental key in determining how and when you encounter God. God wants to bring the greatness locked up within you outside so that every body can see and give thanks to God for your life. However, being at the right place at the right time is a vital necessity to encountering God. Why do you think God told Abraham to leave his family and relatives to a place where he will show him? (Genesis 12.1)

God has isolated you from unbeleif and doubt

In essence God was saying, you are in the wrong place and before I can bless you Abram, you need to be in a location where the blessing will not be hampered by those who are close to you. Hence, I want you to leave this place and I will show you a location where it will be conducive to bless you so that the blessing will be maintained and sustained (Genesis 12.1-2).

God is talking to you about your association

If you are reading this now, you are destined for greatness but you must be willing to be emptied off the world so that God can fill you with his glory. You cannot be effective for God if you have issues of the past. A baggage of the past could be a guilt of things done badly in the past or any other forms of impurities.

Moses was in this situation, he left from being in a palace where life was comfortable and wonderful, to being in a place where he owned nothing. That is why God wanted to deliver Moses from the issues of the past. Moses had low self-esteem, poor self-image, negative self-concept, he was full of fear and his future looked gloomy because he had no great expectations for the future, plus he was isolated from his family.

Don't run ahead of God's programme for your life

The promise of becoming a prince in Egypt was ruined because he rushed in life, and ran ahead of God because he had not yet had any personal encounter with God. In all the struggles Moses was experiencing with the baggage of the past, God was using the circumstances of his life to cultivate the greatness he deposited in him before he was born.

The wanted murderer was the deliverer

On the natural side of things, Moses was a wanted murderer but also in this murderer was a red sea opener and a nation changer. God wants to do the same thing for you; he has predestined you to be conformed into the image of his Son.

For whom he did foreknow, he also did predestinate to be conformed to the image of his Son, that he might be the firstborn among many brethren. (Romans 8.29 King James Version)

Become like Christ each day

A truly significant person is an individual who is continually being transformed into the image of the Son of God through prayer and daily application of the word of God. However, all these activities are made possible through solitude. The truth you need to know about isolation is that, it provides an atmosphere conducive for quality communion with God and growth in the knowledge of God. It also gives you an opportunity to exercise your faith and become a stronger and well grounded person in the word of God.

Ask when you need something

Isolation is also a testing time which makes the significant person look at things from God's perspective. It helps to sharpen the spiritual discernment of a significant person. When developing your spiritual vision, it is necessary to be alone with God when God teaches you how to fight the good fight of faith.

Who fed thee in the wilderness with manna, which thy fathers knew not; that he might humble thee, and that he might prove thee, to do thee good at thy latter end: (Deuteronomy 8.16 King James Version)

Reject the labels

Get on problems as they arise

While the season of isolation is a time of divine encounter, it is also a time of coming and confronting the real you so that God changes you into the person you were created to be. When God created you, you were perfect in beauty but your environment, your mental conditioning and negative programming have buried your real self, which is now recognized as the labels society has placed on you.

Break every limits put on you

What people do is that they define you based on what you do or have done. People put limits on you by putting you in a box showing to you that, you cannot go further than this because the people with these labels or names you have can only go this far in life.

Don't accept the status quo

This is the habitation of people who have this label you have and they can amount to nothing in life. Sometimes circumstances in your life remind you of the label people placed on you and make you believe that what people have said is valid and true.

Refuse to give into social pressure

The majority of people have accepted the name society has given them; they have embraced it and received it as their lot in life. But the truth is, all that people have called you is an attempt to bury your limitless possibilities and potential. God has already said, there is no limit to what you can accomplish and you must believe God. Gideon was in the same situation where he had accepted the limits life placed on him. Let us read his story:

See the positive in every negative

And the angel of the LORD appeared unto him, and said unto him, The LORD is with thee, thou mighty man of valour.

And Gideon said unto him, Oh my Lord, if the LORD be with us, why then is all this befallen us? and where be all his miracles which our fathers told us of, saying, Did not the LORD bring us up from Egypt? but now the LORD hath forsaken us, and delivered us into the hands of the Midianites.

And the LORD looked upon him, and said, Go in this thy might, and thou shalt save Israel from the hand of the Midianites: have not I sent thee?

And he said unto him, Oh my Lord, wherewith shall I save Israel? Behold, my family is poor in Manasseh, and I am the least in my father's house.

(Judges 6.11-15 King James Version)

Refuse negative conditioning

As far as God was concerned, Gideon was a mighty man of valour but he saw himself as a victim and had accepted the label as the least family in Manasseh and the youngest son in his family. How many people are exactly like Gideon before an Angel comes and change their wrong mindset about themselves?

You must change your negative way of thinking

This story demonstrates that if you can change people's mindset about themselves, you can change the course of their destiny. As you read this book, recognize the angel or messenger of God sent to you and is speaking to you in the pages of this book. Receive it and change your wrong perspective about your entire existence.

People are suffering from inferiority complex

Most people in life define themselves based on what their parents or other important people in their life have called them. Whenever you accept what people or your close family have called you, you begin to take on the characteristics of that name or label. When you respond to what they call you, you begin to live according to the label placed on you; you act, talk, and behave in that fashion. That is when being isolated becomes crucial because, it is a time of divine visitation and a time of change of name (perspective). The first thing the Angel did was call Gideon by the identity God had ordained before he was born.

Gideon was a mighty warrior in God's thinking

As far as God was concerned, Gideon was a mighty man of war but society had conditioned him and placed a limit on who he was and what he could accomplish in life. However, the result of Gideon receiving God's opinion of his identity led to a change of destiny. When a change of mindset occurs, there is a change in purpose and destiny. Saul is another typical example of one whose name was changed to Paul and that led to a change in purpose and destiny.

Importance of names

The significance of names cannot be underestimated. Names in the Bible were given by men based on the circumstances surrounding the birth of an individual (Genesis 41:51). However, God gave names according to the purpose why that person was to exist. The name Jesus is a Hebrew word meaning Yeshua, (Jehovah saves). A name then from God's perspective is associated with destiny and the reason why a thing or a person exists. If God the creator gave names based on the function of a person in his divine plan then how much more we?

Name determines your programming and destiny

We see in the life of Jacob this principle that governs 'name' in motion. The name Jacob means supplanter or deceiver and what do we see or what characteristic does Jacob display in the Bible? A deceiver! Jacob acted out his name by deceiving his father.

From the example of Jacob, it can be said that, God was teaching us something about the significance of names.

Your name determines your character

According to Dr. Abraham Chigbundu "whatever you are called, that is what you are."[3] The question at this moment is what is your name? Could it be that you require a change of name? Before you change, you must ask yourself if your current location in life is as a result of the name that has been given you either by your parents or adopted parents.

Your name can limit your potential

Some people have been held in bondage through the names given to them by society. What name have you been called by those around you? Is that name pulling you down or bringing you up? Honesty is the key to your name being changed by God. When you are honest with yourself, you acknowledge your problem to God by telling him your weakness and your name. This reminds me of the Jabez prayer.

1 Chronicles 4.9-10 (New Living Translation)

There was a man named Jabez who was more honorable than any of his brothers. His mother named him Jabez because his birth had been so painful. And Jabez called on the God of Israel, saying, Oh that thou wouldest bless me indeed, and enlarge my coast, and that thine hand might be with me, and that thou wouldest keep me from evil, that it may not grieve me! And God granted him that which he requested.

When Jabez recognized that his name was not making him productive in life, though he was more honourable than his brethren. He called on God and requested for God to give him a solution to his problem and God granted it to him. If God has done it for Jabez, he will do the same for you. He is waiting for you to ask in faith.

Eliminate the spirit of pride

If you are a person reading this book and have inherited the name 'pride', you need to tell God how arrogant you are and as you acknowledge it, the hand of God will be activated to change you from an arrogant person into a humble individual.

Avoid making this costly mistake

A significant person could have found themselve in a situation where they were honest about their true condition but instead of speaking to Jesus about it,

---

[3]   Dr. Abraham Chigbundu, Loose Him And Let Him Go (Benin City: Voice of freedom publications, 2000), 52

they made the dreadful mistake of spreading it around to gossipers who took it to gossip about them.

Earnestly seek God's face

As an individual who is passionate about change, the only person who has the power is God and his word. God will like you to come before him naked, remove every mask, pretence and hypocrisy. God knows the real you and he desires to help you discover your real self and make you a man or woman of destiny. By you openly acknowledging your names (sins), you give God the licence to move in your life to turn things around. A broken and a contrite heart God will not reject.

Get ready for a divine visitation

In Genesis 32.24, 28, Jacob had a visitation from the Angel of the Lord that changed his destiny forever. Before he was visited, he was alone.

Then Jacob was left alone; and a Man wrestled with him until the breaking of day. Then he said, "Let me go, for the dawn is breaking." But he said, I will not let you go unless you bless me." So he said to him, "What is your name?" And he said, "Jacob." He said, "Your name shall no longer be Jacob, but Israel; for you have striven with God and with men and have prevailed."

Jacob's problem was his name

The significance of this single event in Jacob's life cannot be underestimated. He asked the Angel to bless him but all the Angel did was 'changed his name'. So all his life, Jacob's problem was the name he was given when he was born. How many people do you know who are suffering because of the poor decision of their parents in giving a bad name to their child? This was the major turning point in Jacob's life. This particular event teaches a powerful principle of isolation: "There is no revelation without isolation."

God isolates you to bless you

You might not have understood why God has been removing some friends out of your life. The reason is to isolate you for a supernatural habitation and visitation.

Dominate your flesh

God does not want you operating by your five senses, he wants you walking and living by faith and the only thing that is holding you from walking in the spirit is your flesh (the five senses). God has already made it clear that; they that are in the flesh cannot please him (Romans 8.13). When the flesh is subdued, then you have just qualified for the next level of preparation.

You are on a journey of discovery

In his series on operating in the anointing, Benny Hinn points out the four symbolic locations and their significance to the believer. "He talks about Gilgal which means "rolling away." This is the place of growing up. It is a place we become grounded in the word. Bethel means "the house of God" and this is the place of crucifixion. After you have passed the test at Bethel, you are now ready for Jericho, which is "the place of warfare".

Jericho is where you put on the whole armour of God and it is a place where God shows up and is ready to fight all your battles. Since the Angel wrestled with Jacob at Bethel, this is where the flesh was subdued in Jacob and he began to live in the spirit. Finally, Jordan is "the place of vision", it is the place you see the Lord"[2].

> I am crucified with Christ: nevertheless I live; yet not I, but Christ liveth in me: and the life which I now live in the flesh I live by the faith of the Son of God, who loved me, and gave himself for me. (Galatians 2.20 King James Version)

Jacob's honesty rewarded

By answering the Angel, Jacob faced who he was; he acknowledged his true nature – a deceiver, and immediately after facing who he was, the Angel of the Lord changed his name to Israel meaning "Prince with God."

Principle of salvation is revealed

The second principle revealed from this passage is that, God will always change a person who comes before him naked. When you confront who you are, God will change you into a new person. When a sinner becomes conscious of the reality of their true condition, God is moved with compassion to change that person into the original person they were created to be (2 Corinthians 5.17). They become a "new brand person".

You are the architect of your destiny

Romans 10.10

For it is by believing in your heart that you are made right with God, and it is by confessing with your mouth that you are saved.

In essence, Jacob was saying Lord, this is the name I was given and it has made me who I am today. But God said, I have given you the name that I had when I created you in eternity before time began. I created you, you were perfect in beauty and I called you by name, I called you 'Prince with God.'

Come before God naked

Facing who you are includes taking the label you have been given to God and asking God to give you the original you, the one he had in mind when he created you before time begun. Before you stepped into time, God had already finished everything concerning you in eternity. He had already pre-determined the paths you are to take in time and your destination was set in advance before you were born.

Ephesians 1.4

. . . Even as [in His love] He chose us [actually picked us out for Himself as His own] in Christ before the foundation of the world, that we should be holy (consecrated and set apart for Him) and blameless in His sight, even above reproach, before Him in love. (Amplified Bible)

God will restore your wasted years

When you spend time with the wrong people and share your problems with them, depending on that individual, they can sympathize with you, gossip about you, laugh at you or do something about it if they can. However, sharing your problems with God during your time of isolation will enable God to make you whole – nothing missing and nothing broken in your life. When you know the truth about yourself, that is when true repentance begins and when God ministers healing to you. With some the process to restoration is slow but others experience instantaneous healing.

Benefit of Isolation

The season of isolation will cause you to accurately assess your true identity. Since who you are determines what you do with your life, it is vital that you seek God with a determined attitude in his word to discover who you truely are. It all comes down to how you handle or understand the seasons in your life.

Isolation is a season of learning and growing

The principle of isolation teaches us that it is part of God's plan to be alone so that you can have fellowship with the Lord. It is impossible to go deeper in the things of God when you are constantly giving the area of your life that belongs to God to friends. The first step then is to identify the season of your life and then let God work on you to establish what is lacking in your faith.

God's ability has become your ability

In the season of isolation, the significant person learns to lean on God and his word. He realises that, his own strength and abilities are limited so he or she embraces God's strength and abilities. There are people who fail in life because, they put confidence in the arm of the flesh. However, your strength and abilities can bring you to a certain extent in life. There will come a point in your life where your confidence and abilities will cease to serve you.

This is your season of exercising your faith

Don't wait for that to happen, begin developing your confidence and trust in God and his word. As you grow and develop in the word, your season of isolation will turn into a season of productivity. This is because, your level of maturity will increase and hence a change in your level of responsibility.

Chapter summary

You are no longer a victim

There is no doubt that there has been a thorough discussion in this chapter on the principle of Isolation. The challenge of isolation has been carefully examined. It has been observed that, it is in one sense a tool used by God to change our self-image and a tool for building our self-esteem. This season is absolutely important because it helps us to stop focusing on what is wrong with us; it enables us to see ourselves as God sees us in his word.

God is training you to be like him

During isolation, God wrestles with us until our flesh is wrestled out of us, meaning we stop living based on the dictates of our senses. We are free from serving ourselves to become servants of God.

You have sufficient grace to grow and mature

It was also seen that, isolation is an opportunity for a man or woman of significance to re-examine his life so that he may change whatever needs to be corrected. While an individual was depending on her or his own abilities, through isolation a significant person learns how to depend on God and yield to his leading. Isolation is a season in your life where God reveals the true you to yourself (the version of you created by society negative programming) so that he can enable you to become a new brand person in Christ. This is the person you were meant to be from an eternal perspective. The word of God locates you and then change your state and grant you your estate.

BREAKING IN — AND BREAKING OUT

And behold, you will conceive in your womb and bear a son, and you shall name Him Jesus. (Luke 1.31 King James Version)

*I*n this chapter, the challenge of breaking in to break out is the subject matter of our study. Before we go into this subject, let's examine the following analogy which will enable us to understand the concept in this chapter.

When a woman who was once in a state of freedom from pregnancy became pregnant with a baby, there has been an invasion in her body.

After a woman conceives in her womb, everything in her body changes, in order to enable the young foetus in her womb to grow.

Know what you are carrying

A woman, who is pregnant, has her priority changed as a result of her baby. Her focus now becomes inwardly projected with the new life within. Everything she does to her body does not only affect her but also her baby.

Protect your baby

This analogy describes accurately the essence of this chapter. This chapter looks into the period when the significant person incubated their vision and begins to pursue what God has placed in them. What is the significance of the term "breaking in"?

Go after your dreams and visions

A time of breaking in is a time when an individual receives or discovers their vision in life. It is also a time when an individual steps into the path and the right lane that leads to their destiny. As soon as an individual breaks in, their life takes on a new meaning. However, breaking out is vital for breaking into the path to your destiny and we will also discuss the principle of break out as well.

> "For nothing will be impossible with God."
> And Mary said, "Behold, the bondslave of the Lord; may it be done to
> me according to your word." And the angel departed from her (Luke 1.37,
> 38 King James Version).

Nurture and cultivate your vision

This was the moment Mary broke-in into the path to her destiny when she accepted the word of the Lord. In the same way Mary's life changed as soon as she received the word of God concerning her purpose in life, so also will it be unto you when you accept God's vision for your life. Always remember that a new vision needs a new location where it can be nurtured, nourished, protected and cultivated in order to make it grow. A new vision also requires new associations to keep it alive.

Select who to associate and spend time with carefully

> "And behold, even your relative Elizabeth has also conceived a son in her
> old age; and she who was called barren is now in her sixth month. (Luke
> 1.36 King James Version)

As a person with a vision, you cannot afford to associate with those who have no vision for their lives. The Angel recommended Elizabeth to Mary because he knew that, Elizabeth had a similar vision and together, they could comfort each other and inspire each other in their way to fulfilling their individual destiny.

Now at this time Mary arose and went in a hurry to the hill country, to a city of Judah. And entered the house of Zacharias and greeted Elizabeth (Luke 1.39, 40 King James Version).

Recognize the divine connection God has sent

God is going to link you up with the right people who will enable the fulfilment of your vision. When the right person comes you will know because the spirit in you will be the same spirit in them.

But having the same spirit of faith, according to what is written, "I believe, therefore I spoke," we also believe, therefore we also speak, (2 Corinthians 4.13 King James Version).

This is how you will recognize the right people who God has sent to support you during your vision. You will be speaking the same language because you are of the same spirit.

Look at this principle from other angles

The significance of the time of breaking in then can be identified in many different angles. A time of breaking in may be identified when an individual has come to a place in their life where God becomes their central focus. A place of breaking in may also be used to refer to a transitional period in the life of a significant person where he has to face a challenge which is threatening to prevent him or her from entering into the next season of his or her life.

To enter your next season, you will face resistance

Mary experienced a time where she was in danger of being stoned to death by her society because the law demanded that whoever blasphemes God will be stoned to death (Leviticus 24.13). Can you imagine Mary accusing God for impregnating her to her husband Joseph? Instead of attempting to argue with Mary or exposing her for commiting adultery, he decided to put her out of his house secretly because he never believed anything Mary said to him. He knew that, if he exposed her, she was going to be stoned to death. That is how serious the law was concerning any one who commited adultery.

Mary in danger of being stoned

To add insult to injury, she blamed God for her pregnancy which would have generated more problems for her by the pharisees and teachers of the law. It was not easy for Mary but because God's hand was in it, he intervened in the situation and turned things around for good. When God's hand is on your life, no matter the persecution, you will always come out victoriously. The vision God has given for your future will come under severe attack but you should be assured that, it was God who gave it to you in the first place and he will see to it that, it is fulfilled. The proof that God's hand is on your life is that, you attract lots of challenges.

This is how the birth of Jesus the Messiah came about: His mother Mary was pledged to be married to Joseph, but before they came together, she was found to be pregnant through the Holy Spirit (Matthew 1.18 New living Translation)

The voice you heard is genuine

You heard a voice which gave you a vision about the great things God intends to do through you but only you heard the voice so when you tell others, they find it hard to believe you.

"So then, King Agrippa, I was not disobedient to the vision from heaven (Acts 26.19)

You are about to be promoted

The season of breaking-in is absolutely a significant moment in the life of a significant person for several reasons. This season also denotes that promotion is at hand but in order to obtain that promotion it is required that preparation be carried out in his or her life. In order to break-in, acquiring knowledge then becomes a prerequisite in the process of breaking-in.

Increase your level of knowledge

By gaining quality information, you are aware of what belongs to you as a child of God. By gaining revelational knowledge in ever increasing measure, you will know why God has placed you over the works of his hand. There are lots of people in positions of authority but they lack the understanding of the reason behind the power they have been entrusted with. Ignorance of the purpose of authority results in abuse of authority. Instead of it being use for the betterment of others, they use it to the destruction of themselves and others.

Sharpen your discernment on spiritual realities

Another reason for this season is to teach you how the enemy operates. The entire operational system of the enemy is exposed so that you will comprehend what makes the devil have access to a person's life. You will know how he works and what he is using to destroy people's life.

The devil is a master at destroying people's life but his strategies are so hidden that many are unaware of his tactics and others are unaware of his schemes.

Fight the good fight of faith

The first deception of the enemy is to make you believe that there are no enemies. Since Satan operates from darkness, his victims are first drawn into darkness and then being in darkness, they are blinded by the darkness and that's when the devil moves in to steal, kill and destroy (John 10.10). Leaving his victims utterly ruined and helpless, the devil quickly moves to the next victim and it all begins with ignorance.

Give no opportunity to your enemy

But thank God for the season of breaking in, because an opportunity is given to the significant person to have a working knowledge of the devil. The reason why God says "be sober, be vigilant, because your enemy the devil walks about like a roaring lion seeking whom he may devour" (1 Peter 5.8) is to teach us how the enemy is restless until he destroys a person's life.

Stand your ground like a mighty soldier

Being aware of the operation of the devil is vitally important in this day and age because he is working overtime to destroy anyone who has given him access into his life. Sin, no matter how minute it might be is the doorway to which Satan comes into an individual's life to destroy everything that concerns them.

The main reason many are not aware of the enemy's operation is because they are being ruled by their five senses. In order to know the enemy activities you must have a daily prayer life. The battle you and I are involved in is a spiritual battle.

Immense yourself in the word daily

To fight a spiritual battle, you have to understand how to live and be controlled by the Holy Spirit. If you do not embark on the journey of walking in the spirit, you will not fulfill your potential and destiny. Further information on how to walk in the realm of the spirit will be covered in a later chapter. Your potential will not be fully realised if you are not knowledgeable about the operation of the devil.

The battle is over your divine destiny

The battle you are engaged in is a battle over your destiny and your soul as well. Your soul is made up of your mind or intellect, emotion and your will. The devil wants to access you on every available voice: the media, the newspapers, the internet and close friends, family members and relatives.

If they are not under the leadership of the Holy Ghost, they are open to the other options. The devil wants to get to your mind, he wants to shape the way you think and if he is successful, he is able to control your life. The devil uses these mediums of communication to get your attention in order to distract you.

Come out and be Holy

While God intends to purify you from the pollution of sin, the devil wants to poison you with sin so that he can render you ineffective and unproductive. Sin causes you to be weak and fearful, it weakens and poisons the power of God on your life, it brings with it guilt, disgrace, frustration, emotional torments, condemnation and shame to name a few.

Sin produces death

The result of sin is death of something in your life. Whenever the devil detects that there is going to be a break-in in your life, while the enemy is monitoring your progress and sees that you are about to move up higher, he devises strategies to break your focus and distract you so that you cannot break in. However you need to become aware that unless you give him access, he cannot stop you from breaking-in.

The enemy gains access in your life through sin

The devil could not stop Moses from breaking – in into the world but he planned to kill him immediately after he was delivered from his mother's womb.

> Then the king of Egypt spoke to the Hebrew midwives, one of whom was named Shiphrah and the other was named Puah;
>
> And he said, "When you are helping the Hebrew women to give birth and see them upon the birthstool, if it is a son, then you shall put him to death; but if it is a daughter, then she shall live." (Exodus 1.15-16 King James Version)

Breaking in – into the presence

When dealing with the concept of breaking in, it is important to note that, there are different dimensions to it. The concept of breaking-in can also be viewed from a worship stand-point. Enjoying the presence of God requires breaking-in; activate the presence by singing and making melody in your heart to the Lord. (Ephesians 5.18) You can start by speaking in tongues (Jude 1.20). To experience his presence some take thirty minutes to become conscious of his presence. It all depends on each individual's relationship with the Holy Spirit. The good news is every one has access to the throne room of grace. Therefore let us draw near with confidence to the throne of grace, so that we may receive mercy and find grace to help in time of need." (Hebrews 4.16 King James Version)

You are a holy child of God

The next place where every born again child has access is the holy place and ultimately to the holy of holy or the most holy place. The word says, without holiness no one can see the Lord,

> Pursue peace with all men, and the sanctification without which no one will see the Lord. (Hebrews 12.14)

> But like the Holy One who called you, be holy yourselves also in all your behavior; because it is written, you shall be Holy, for I am Holy." (1 Peter 1.15-16)

According to Alice Smith, "We who enter the Holy place must refuse to lift up our souls to materialistic idolatery or false ideas about God. We cannot be motivated by fleshly desires and expect to stand in his presence. For God did not call us to be impure but to live a holy life, not diluted and stained by the world (1 Thess. 4.7)[3]."

You are separated unto God for holy purposes

Since without holiness, no one can see the Lord, entering his presence where his holiness is requires purity. Purity of heart is required because the Bible says blessed are the pure in heart for they shall see God (Matthew 5.8 King James Version).

Psalms 24:3, 4:

Who may ascend the hill of the Lord? Who may stand in his holy place? He who has clean hands and a pure heart, who does not lift up his soul to an idol or swear by what is false (New International Version).

Be aware of the division of the temple

There are Christians who are not aware of the division in the temple; the outer court, the inner court and the most holy place. Since the Old Testament was a foreshadow of things to come, we in the New Testament are now the temple of God where God dwells.

You are the temple of God

The Old Testament temple contains a specific pattern that the high priest followed in order to enter and offer sacrifice unto God. The most holy place was reserved for the high priest to enter and offer a sacrifice once every year. When Jesus came, he established a new order through his blood and has made it possible to live daily in the most holy place. As a result of his sacrifice, he has made the most holy place accessible to all those who will accept his sacrifice.

The Goal of prayer

Breaking-in and abiding then in the most holy place should be the goal of prayer. How do you break-in? I have experienced the most holy place so I can tell you that, it is not difficult at all to break-in but is going to cost you quality time in the presence of God. You need to realise however that God is a jealous God and because he lives in you, he will make sure that you go through the process of sanctification through the word of God so that you will not be committing spiritual adultery with the world (James 1.25), (Acts 20.32).

John 15.3:

> You are already clean because of the word I have spoken to you (New Living Translation)

God desires to reveal his glory

All this process will come naturally as you spend time with God on a daily basis. Most of the processes are taught by the Holy Spirit and through the word of God. If you play your role diligently by spending quality time with the the Lord, God will do his part speedily by revealing his glory in you. (Acts 26.18).

The Outer Court

Every time you are praying, you should not be satisfied with the outer court because the presence of God affects your body but it dwells in your spirit. When you keep your body pure from the pollution of the sins of the flesh, you are preparing the foundation for an effective prayer life. (1 Corinthians 6.19)

The Inner Court

The next location to prepare for an effective prayer experience is the inner court or your soul. Your soul, which consists of your mind, emotion and will, is where you bless the Lord and this is where you develop the muscles of your focus. Have you ever met people in church who cannot focus during worship sessions? (Psalms 103.1)

His glory is revealed when we worship

They have not learned to develop the muscle of focus. You learn to focus on the Lord alone in your soul. As you praise the Lord, the anointing should saturate your mind and this settles down or quietens your soul and put it at rest. Always remember that your soul thirsts for the living God (Psalms 42.2). Songs of praise are what settles down the activities of the soul and makes it synchronize with your spirit.

The Most Holy Place

Your heart (spirit) and your flesh sing for joy to the living God (Psalms 84.2). As you sing worship songs with your heart, you will activate the presence, which is already residing in you if you are a born again child of God. The more time spent, you will begin to feel something come upon you and that is the anointing which is the fruit of the presence of the Holy Spirit indwelling you.

Learn to activate his glory in your worship

Always note that, the presence of God produces a fruit and that fruit is the power of God. While you have made it to the most holy place, there is more room for advancement. You can offer sacrifice to God through intercessory prayer (Hebrews 13.15). Entering the most holy place is the third dimension of the tabernacle and this is where the presence of God dwells.

Learn to be conscious of the Spirit of God in you

All born again children of God do have access to the presence of God in the most holy place but only few are enjoying the reality of his holiness. This is because only few are willing to pay the price of spending quality time with God in order to develop a deeper intimate understanding of his holiness.

Protect your purity

The secret of dwelling in the most holy place is this: one must not participate in sin or anything that defies the temple of God (Psalms 15). Always remember that the spirit of God in you is the Spirit of Holiness and he desires to give you a deeper understanding of his Holiness . . . . And who through the Spirit of holiness was declared with power to be the Son of God by his resurrection from the dead: Jesus Christ our Lord (Romans 1.4 New Living Translation)

Enjoy the special benefit of walking with God

There are benefits associated with living in the most Holy place. When you enter the most holy place, God pours his love on you and there are instant answers to prayer. When you hear or see a man or a woman of God who receives answers-I mean instant answers to his or her prayer's – you should know that, he or she has learned the secret of living in the most holy place.

Live your life on God's terms

One of the marks of a significant person is their determination to overcome the obstacles that attempt to prevent them from abiding in the most holy place. His ability to overcome distractions is what distinguishes the significant person from those who are satisfied with their present location in their prayer life.

Activities in the Most Holy Place

One significant aspect of the most holy place is that the high priest performs certain activities. Jesus is our high priest and he still performs offering on our behalf. The word says he is the high priest of our confession (Hebrews 3.1) God has called Christians to perform in the office of a priest.

You are God's dwelling place

As intercessors, a significant person understands the value of operating in the third dimension of the tabernacle. Since the Holy Spirit lives in us because of the death and resurrection of Jesus Christ, all born again children of God have the presence of God dwelling in them but not all Christians know how to walk and activate the glory of God residing in them.

The Apostle Paul said,

You carry the throne room everywhere you go

Do you not know that you are a temple of God and that the Spirit of God dwells in you (1 Corinthians 3.16, 17 (New Lving Translation)?

Do you now see that the Spirit of God dwells in us and that brings with it an awesome responsibility? To keep this body as the dwelling place of God, there are negative activities that are totally forbidden because they will pollute God's presence in you.

Learn to activate your spirit and take dominion

Now that God lives in you, breaking-in and activating his presence within us requires fellowshipping with the Holy Spirit and activating his presence in us. Now the division is spirit, soul and body. As you can see, the outer court is your body (Contains your five sensory perceptions); the inner court is your soul (Emotions, mind or intellect and will) is the holy place. The centre court is the most Holy place which is your spirit (heart) is where the presence of God dwells. Your soul also contains your perceptual abilities (intuition, the sixth sense).

Ephesians 5.18: (New living translation)

Don't be drunk with wine, because that will ruin your life. Instead, be filled with the Holy Spirit,

Learn to focus on God with your eyes closed

During worship time, most people do not know how to worship God from their heart. However, you are born again and as a child of God, you have everything within you to enable you to worship God from your heart. Your body is now the dwelling place of God but you need to learn to live and walk in the realm of the spirit which is within you.

2 Corinthians 5.17 (New living translation)

This means that anyone who belongs to Christ has become a new person. The old life is gone; a new life has begun!

Treat your body right

As you are aware that your body is his dwelling place; shouldn't that prompt you to start treating it as if you were only the caretaker of your body? And that is exactly who you are, the custodian of your body. Your body is not your own, it has been bought with a heavy price.

Old Testament Temple

In the Old Testament the priests used to go to the temple to perform sacrifices before entering into the various dimensions of the tabernacle. If the priest performed different rituals before moving from one dimension of the temple to the next, we are also to do similar things.

Live by faith and not by sight

The only difference is that we do it by faith and not by physical activities. We pray by faith. We speak in tongues by faith and we sing and worship God by faith. We also eat the leaven bread, which is symbolic of the word of God.

Hebrews 11.6 (New Living Translation)

And without faith it is impossible to please God, because anyone who comes to him must believe that he exists and that he rewards those who earnestly seek him.

You carry God with you everywhere now

Since our body is now the temple of God, we need to understand the different divisions in our body and then learn to align them with the presence of God. In other words, in order to break-in and remain in the presence of God, we need to be conscious of the Holy Spirit living in us. By being God's conscious, or by being God inside minded, it will enable us to keep things before us that only promote the holiness and righteousness of God in our lives.

Therefore, I urge you, brothers, in view of God's mercy, to offer your bodies as living sacrifices, holy and pleasing to God – this is your spiritual act of worship. (Romans 12.1 (New Living Translation)

Breaking-out

This is where the concept of breaking out comes in handy to make you aware of the things that will pollute the holiness of God in you if you allow them. There is a need to break out of the ties of this world.

Live a separate and purposeful life

Any unholy attachment with this world has to be broken in order to be purified and come to a place where you can enjoy intimacy with your Father. In order to successfully break out from this world and its influence, you have to be determined to develop friendship with God through prayer and renewing of the mind by the word of God.

Learn to meditate until you become the word at work

James 4.4 (New International Version)

You adulterous people, don't you know that friendship with the world is hatred toward God? Anyone who chooses to be a friend of the world becomes an enemy of God.

This should be done through quality time in the presence of God. According to James, "any friendship with the world is enmity with God" (James 3.12). Any relationship with the world system (lawlessness) has to be terminated because the influence of the world is intensely overwhelming and if an individual wants to please God and fulfil their destiny, it is vital that they keep themselves clean by associating with clean people. People who are dirty will dirty you.

Be not deceived: evil communications corrupt good manners. (1Corinthians 15.33 King James Version)

Protect God's presence at all cost

Negative actions and words are what poison the presence of God in you. Since where sin is the presence of God is not, it is crucial that you are not found where sin is at any time but if you do, you need to flee.

Ephesians 4.30:

And do not grieve the Holy Spirit of God, with whom you were sealed for the day of redemption (New Living Translation)

Pursue your dreams

In pursuing a God given vision, breaking ties with the world is a prerequisite. You have to be free from the elements of the world if you are to truly make God's dream for your life a tangible reality. In order to break out from this world system of operation, it is important to know what the world is attempting to sell to you. The world's ultimate intention is to control your life through your thoughts.

Come therefore from among them and be ye separated and I will receive you. (2 Corinthians 7.8 (King James Version)

Since what you think determines your identity, and who you are determines your behaviour, the world wants to negatively programme your mind to think wrong thoughts and when you think wrong thoughts, those wrong thoughts create your self-image and since who you are determines your behaviour, you begin to act on your negative programming and eventually find yourself on the wrong path.

Put simply, your self-esteem determines the way you act or carry yourself. The wrong thought patterns are reflected in your self-image (the way you see yourself) and your negative self-image produces feelings of low self-esteem (a feeling that you are worthless).

Focus on God's word

If the world can succeed in feeding you the wrong information it can succeed in controlling your destiny. The wrong information when received produces a wrong frame of mind (your negative interpretation of reality) and a negative mindset determines your behaviour and your behaviour determines your destiny and destiny determines legacy.

For as he thinketh in his heart, so is he . . . (Proverbs 23.7 (King James Version).

If you give your mind to the world, they will feed it until they begin to dictate how you think; fear and wrong actions will be the end result. While the world is attempting to socially programme you in order to destroy your destiny, God on the other hand desires to reprogramme your mind for success and good health.

Do not conform to the pattern of this world, but be transformed by the renewing of your mind. Then you will be able to test and approve what God's will is – his good, pleasing and perfect will. (Romans 12.2 (New International version)

You are the one with the power

It is vital to note also that as a personal representative of God on this planet earth, you are in charge. As people of God, anything that goes wrong on this planet is our fault. We have a high position with God and we need to exercise our authority at all times to dismantle the works of the devil.

> Thou shalt also decree a thing, and it shall be established unto thee: and the light shall shine upon thy ways (Job 22.28 (King James Version).

You determine what happens in your life from now on

The Lord Jesus Christ has defeated this world and since Jesus did it for us, we have no business allowing the world to rule or control us. We need to use our faith filled words to tame the elements of nature. The world and sin has ceased to be a threat because it has been defeated.

Sin shall not be a problem no longer because it has been defeated. The devil has lost his power and he is void of authority and power to lord it over you.

You have the control and the influence

Failure has ceased to be a problem because it has been defeated. The devil is completely paralysed and a total failure. Now that we have been separated and made the righteousness of God in Christ Jesus, we are now the sons of God with rights and previleges (2 Corinthians 5.21). Since you have no more excuses to why you could not fulfil your destiny, get up and fulfil all your dreams in Jesus name Amen.

And having disarmed the powers and authorities, he made a public spectacle of them, triumphing over them by the cross (Colossians 2.15 (New International Version).

THE SPIRITUAL VERSUS THE NATURAL

If we live in the Spirit, let us also walk in the Spirit. (Galatians 5.25)

*T*o live in three realms, one has to be willing to make a quality decision to learn how to live in them. There are two major realms, the natural realm and the realm of the spirit. The next realm is the intellectual realm. The Apostle was speaking to the Galatians about the natural realm where our body lives and the spiritual realm in which our spirit functions.

Operate from a spiritual standpoint

He talks about the continual struggle that goes on between our body and our spirit. The flesh (The five senses) desires to rule our lives and our spirit also wants to rule as well. This battle is actually intensified when you got born again because for the first time in the history of your life, your spirit has come alive or has been recreated (2 Corinthians 5.17). But your spiritual senses are not yet developed properly to transcend your physical senses.

Dominate your physical senses with your spirit

Before then your flesh was the master that dominated your life and you followed the inclination and the passions of your body because you were disconnected from

God through disobedience. The master that determined the course of your life was your five senses. However, when you got born again, your new, born again spirit and the Holy Spirit living in you want to take over your life and help you fulfil your destiny easily and effortlessly by dominating your body.

For the flesh lusts against the Spirit, and the Spirit against the flesh: and these things are opposed one to the other, that ye should not do those things which ye desire; (Galatians 5.17 (Darby bible Translation).

Aim at functioning from your spirit

The truth is, a truly successful Christian is one who is not satisfy with their present location and is always striving to live in the Spirit. Kingdom living is in the spiritual dimension of life. Living life from a spiritual point of view makes you a successful Christian.

Your origin is supernatural

Humans in their original design and fashion were not created to live life ruled by their five senses. When you see what is happening in the world presently, you will find that, it is essentially due to the malfunctioning of humanity. Humans were not meant to live and be dominated by their five senses.

Sin is defeated now

The sin factor is what brought about the switch from living in the realm of the spirit (the realm governed by the word of God) to living in the realm governed by the five senses, the realm dominated by ignorance. The five senses consist of what you hear, feel, taste, see, and smell.

Sin is the root cause of problems in the world

When sin (lawlessness) caused man to begin to experience all sorts of troubles and misfortune in their daily lives, the devil took full advantage over man's spiritual blindness (ignorance of God's laws) and ruled him from the five sense gates (man was enslaved to his five senses). The reason men are creating more problems for themselves today than can be solved is because they are governed by their five senses. (The sense realm is ruled by the man of lawlessness).

Apply God's principles in your life

The devil uses ignorance to rule the system he set up in this natural realm) to dominate the world. That is why God says, my people are destroyed (crushed) because of lack of "knowledge" (Hosea 4.6). Knowlege is symbolic of "light" and "ignorance" is symbolic of darkness. As Christians, we are children of light (meaning children of the word of God). The devil is the Prince of darkness. That means that, we should never walk in darkness regarding any situation we face.

1 John 2.15-17 (English Standard Version)

> Do not love the world or the things in the world. If anyone loves the world, the love of the Father is not in him. For all that is in the world – the desires of the flesh and the desires of the eyes and pride in possessions – is not from the Father but is from the world. And the world is passing away along with its desires, but whoever does the will of God abides forever.

Discover your inheritance

Jesus destiny was about restoring men back to their spiritual position (The position of faith, authority, dominion and power). In order to truly have dominion or in order for men to carry out their God given purpose, destiny and dominion mandate, they can only do so by living and being governed by their spirit. It was the spirit of man that was given the dominion mandate and not the flesh or the five senses. In fact the body is the house in which your spirit lives and functions. The home of your spirit is your body and your body contains your five senses.

Build Your Spirit man

Acts 20.32 (New Living Translation)

> "Now I commit you to God and to the word of his grace, which can build you up and give you an inheritance among all those who are sanctified.

The spirit of man, which is also referred to as the inner man in (Ephesians 3.14) has to be built in order for it to dominate the flesh. Your spirit has to gain the control in the spiritual realm in order to subdue the realm ruled by the five sensory perceptions.

You have the spirit of dominion

When Jesus restored man back to their new and beautiful status of power, he was telling us that, you couldn't truly carry out your dominion assignment on earth while being governed by your senses. Your flesh (five sensory perceptions) and your body were originally intended to be your earth suit or the house of your spirit. Your senses were not given to you to rule your spirit but your five senses were given to you to regulate your body, so that you can have the ability to live on this planet and fulfil your destiny.

2 Corinthians 5.7 (New International Version)

> We live by faith, not by sight

God designed us to have authority in three realms, the realm of the spirit, and the aspect of the soul (emotion or feelings, mind or intellect and will or decision maker) and the realm of the natural. The five sensory perceptions consists of what you see (sight), what you hear, what you feel, what you smell and what you taste

Rule your physical senses by developing your spirit

All these five senses enable you to relate with this dimension of reality (the natural realm). However, the spirit of man is intended to regulate the realm of the soul and the five senses of the body. In order for the spirit of man to rule as intended by God, it has to be connected with God. The Holy Spirit plays a vital role in this union because it is the Holy Spirit that unites the spirit of man back to the Spirit of God.

Now you have authority in three realms

The Holy Ghost who is the governor of the kingdom of God united Adam with God. It is faith which is the medium by which Adam function and received instructions for his dominion assignment. That spiritual connection of faith was designed for man to be connected to the realm of the spirit. God lives in the realm governed by the Holy Ghost (eternity) – and so Adam could receive divine instructions through his spirit through the spiritual connector of faith and carry out his dominion mandate. Man has the power to make things happen in the spirit, on the earth and in the intellectual realm.

You are the righteousness of God

Hence, one could say that, the fall of man was a departure of the glory of God. It was through the Holy Spirit (which was living in Adam) that enabled him to fellowship with God and received divine instructions for his dominion assignment.

Romans 3.23 (New International Version)

> for all have sinned and fall short of the glory of God,

You are now in Zion, the city of God

When man disconnected from God resulting in spiritual death (a person without the Holy Spirit is spiritually disconnected from God), they became connected to Satan (the spirit of death) through the spiritual connector of fear. The devil instead of the Holy Spirit begun to control their five senses. So it was their soul, spirit and five sensory perceptions that was distorted The word has let us know that, the children of the senses are not the children of God. In other words those dominated by their five sensory perceptions are not the children of God because they are slaves to Satan.

You are now in Christ, the anointed in his anointing

The spirit of man in the new birth was recreated; it became a new born baby that needs to grow by the nourishment of the word of God and exercise of faith until it becomes a full fledged grown adult man in the spirit before it can rule. That is why the Apostle Peter through the Spirit teaches about the importance of feeding your spirit.

Grow up in your salvation

Like newborn babies, crave pure spiritual milk, so that by it you may grow up in your salvation (1 Peter 2.2 (New International Version).

Learn to talk and behave like the King's kid

The part of your soul which is the mind or intellect need to be reprogrammed by the word, because it did not get born again during the new birth. Your mind contains the negative information and negative programming of the world.

Romans 12.2(New International Version)

Do not conform any longer to the pattern of this world, but be transformed (transfigured) by the renewing of your mind. Then you will be able to test and approve what God's will is – his good, pleasing and perfect will.

God's capacity is your capacity

Without renewing your mind or intellect, the dream of ruling is far out of reach and it can only be made possible when you change the way you think. It only takes a person whose mind is truely renewed to know who they are and carry out the dominion mandate to its fullest maximum capacity.

Spend time in the word daily to think like God

A spiritual baby does not have the ability and capabilities to handle kingdom resources and responsibilities. On the other hand, a truly spiritual mature man or woman is not dominated by their flesh; he or she has learned to dominate the five senses. In other words, he or she has subdued the five senses due to his or her habitual act of exercising themselve unto godliness.

1Timothy 4.7-8 (Amplified Bible)

But refuse and avoid irreverent legends (profane and impure and godless fictions, mere grandmothers' tales) and silly myths, and express your disapproval of them. Train yourself toward godliness (piety), [keeping yourself spiritually fit].

> For physical training is of some value (useful for a little), but godliness (spiritual training) is useful and of value in everything and in every way, for it holds promise for the present life and also for the life which is to come.

Take control over your body

> But [like a boxer] I buffet my body [handle it roughly, discipline it by hardships] and subdue it, for fear that after proclaiming to others the Gospel and things pertaining to it, I myself should become unfit [not stand the test, be unapproved and rejected as a counterfeit]. (1 Corinthians 9.27 Amplified Bible)

The spiritual man feeds his spirit consistently and he or she is more aware of his spirit than his body. Adam in his original condition or state was more aware of his spirit than his body and the senses that regulated it. That could be the reason he did not notice he had a body until he fell short of the glory of God.

You carry the maximum load of God

When God asked where you are, Adam responded by saying the following: "I heared your voice and I hid myself because I was naked." God asked again, who told you that you were naked (Genesis 3.11 (New International Version)? Have you eaten from the fruit of the tree that I told you not to eat of? The tree and the fruit eating experience were responsible for Adam's "new awareness" of his nakedness. Nakedness then can be said to be a result of doing what God told you not to do.

Pursue the word

God has made his headquarters in you

The thing that should happen to us as we pursue God is more awareness of the superiority of our spirit man above our body or earth suit. This should happen to every believer who intends to carry out his or her dominion mandate on earth. You should be growing so strong in the word that, you are more conscious of your spirit. The constituent of your spirit is the word of God!

God's destiny for you is powerful

This is exactly what God intended for us in the death and resurrection of Jesus Christ. God created your spirit man and placed it in a physical body or an earth suit. So our body is actually the house in which we live. It is the house that enables us and gives the legal right to exist as free moral agents to fulfil our dominion mandate on earth. To be controlled by our body (with its five sensory perceptions) is in reality a deviation from God's original intention of the purpose of the body and its five senses.

Your body is your house

To allow the flesh (The five senses) to rule is actually affirming the reign of Satan over a person's existence and purpose. But living to please Satan is not wise because the devil's ultimate agenda is to destroy your body through your senses. No wonder God points out the following: to be carnally minded (your mind dominated by your senses) produces death but to be spiritually minded is life and peace. (Romans 8.6 King James Version) He also says the children of the mind (intellect) and of the flesh (five sensory perceptions) are not the children of God. The children of the word are the children of God. In other words, those who are enslaved to their mind and five sensory perceptions are not operating under God's authority and God's protection.

Romans 8.8

So then they that are in the flesh cannot please God (King James Version).In other words, if you allow your five senses to rule and dominate you, you are living in disobedience to God. You are to allow your obedience to be complete!

And we will be ready to punish every act of disobedience, once your obedience is complete (2 Corinthians 10.6 (New International Version).

Walking in the realm of the spirit

Develop the real you

To function properly in the realm of the spirit, you have to be willing to invest in your spirit man. You have to be willing to build your faith. Feeding on the word of God (spiritual diet) releases spiritual nutrients and that is translated into a spiritual energy in your spirit called faith and this strengthens your spirit to grow and develop spiritual muscles. Your spirit is a spiritual container and it needs faith to keep getting stronger and bigger.

Have intimacy with God's word daily

As you hear and apply the word of God correctly, you are creating a capacity for more of the word of God and you are developing your spiritual container. As you feed your spirit, you are rightly positioning your spirit man to be all that God intended it to be. As your spirit grows and matures, it will begin to dominate your physical senses and as this begins to happen, your spiritual senses will begin to get stronger and begin to dominate your five senses.

> Having been begotten again, not of corruptible seed, but of incorruptible, through the word of God, which liveth and abideth for ever (1 Peter 1.23 American Standard Version).

This scripture is very instructive as it points out what our new identity in Christ consists of. We are the "born word of word." As you are now the "born word of God," your very existence as the born word is dependent on your nourishment by the word of God.

But Jesus told him, "No! The Scriptures say,

> 'People do not live by bread alone, but by every word that comes from the mouth of God (Matthew 4.4 New Living Translation). Man should live by every rhema (the word of God for the now) that comes from God's mouth every day. Your spirit needs to hear from God everyday to feel happy.

The Realm and the Vision

Do you know that the spiritual mature man has a spiritual vision?

> While we look not at the things which are seen, but at the things which are not seen: for the things which are seen are temporal; but the things which are not seen are eternal. (2 Corinthians 4.18 New American Standard Bible)

Pay no attention to what you see

The Apostle Paul speaking by the spirit says we should not look at the things that do appear because; things that are seen (by physical sight or vision) are temporal, meaning they have no eternal value. It also means, they are subject to be changed.

You are God manifested in the flesh

But the things that are not seen (requires spiritual vision to see them) are eternal, meaning they have eternal and lasting value. However the things that are not seen require spiritual vision to see them and walk in them. The man or woman who operates by the word of God sees things from a spiritual point of view and this enables him to develop a spiritual vision that enables him to see (spiritual sight) beyond the physical realm. He or she knows that, beyond this natural realm, there is a spiritual realm that is more real than this natural realm. The word of God has the ability to develop your spiritual sight (vision)

Live and be conscious of your spirit everyday

The man of the spirit knows that, it was a spiritual Supreme Being who lives in the spirit world who decided to create man and placed him in an earthly suit (the body) and placed him in the natural realm. Above all, he or she is aware that, the realm of the spirit is more powerful than this natural realm because it regulates and maintains it.

Live the transcendent life

Walking in the spirit realm and operating by the principles of the word of God enables him or her to put things in an accurate perspective (spiritual perspective). Central to his or her understanding is their awareness that, what takes place in the natural realm is a direct reflection of what has already occurred in the realm of the spirit.

Take advantage of your spiritual discernment

The spiritual man then uses his spiritual vision to see his or her need to exercise in the things of the spirit in order to train his spiritual senses to discern between what is good and what is bad. He or she knows that, according to the law of sin and death, an act of unrighteousness always results in the death of something knowingly or unknowingly.

For everyone who lives on milk is still a baby and does not yet know the difference between right and wrong. But strong meat belongeth to them that are of full age, *even* those who by reason of use have their senses exercised to discern both good and evil. (Hebrews 5.13-14 International Standard Version)

You are now God's agent of change

He also knows that, according to the law of the spirit of life, an act or deed of righteousness will result in life either knowingly or unknowingly (Galatians 6.7). The Bible says, the deeds of a man's hand shall return to him (Proverbs 12.14). For whatsoever good a man does, the same shall he receive from the Lord. An act in the natural will provoke or activate an equal reaction in the spiritual realm. (Ephesians 6.8)

> A man will be satisfied with good by the fruit of his words, and the deeds of a man's hands will return to him. (Proverbs 12.14 New American Standard Bible)

The spiritual man is proactive

God will not do anything for you without your consent or active participation in the process. A spiritual man sees things that carnally minded people cannot see. He or she has divine insights into situations and receives solutions from God's word before the solution manifests in the physical realm. He or she sees things in the Bible in the form of revelational knowledge, which enables him to overcome and solve problems that the natural minded man couldn't discern.

Learn to receive answers to any spiritual or natural problem

They receive answers from the spiritual dimension and bring them to those who need it in the natural realm. A spiritually mature person is one who knows the importance of fellowshipping with God and connecting with him Spirit to spirit. The spiritual mature person hears from God and carries out the instructions accurately.

Become a man or woman with spiritual distinction

A man or a woman on a mission is a spiritual mature person. This kind of mission however, is not ordinary, it is a mission given by God. This person has a working knowledge of the love and the faith of God. They use them if necessary to create a change. They also use them on purpose to solve spiritual problems.

Colossians 3.1-3 (English Standard Version)

> If then ye were raised together with Christ, seek the things that are above, where Christ is, seated on the right hand of God.

Set your mind on the things that are above, not on the things that are upon the earth, for ye died, and your life is hid with Christ in God.

You have the power to become a mature son of God

What the devil is interested in is keeping majority of Christians in the babyhood stage of Christianity because they are weak and vulnerable.

Galatians 5.24 (English Standard Version)

Those who belong to Christ Jesus have crucified (have mortified or subdued their senses) the flesh with its passions and desires.

THE ERA OF DRYNESS

Now Israel loved Joseph more than any of his other sons, because he had been born to him in his old age; and he made a richly ornamented robe for him. (Genesis. 37.1-3 New International Version)

The greater one lives in you

The Era of dryness is a moment where a significant person does not see anything happening in his or her life from a natural stand point. The characteristic of a dry season is noticed or observed in the life of a significant person when he or she feels frustrated. Dryness is a seed sown by the enemy in order to render the significant person ineffective.

Create and maintain your atmosphere

It is also designed to cause a significant individual to dry up. When the significant person experiences dryness, he or she needs to go back to an atmosphere that will remove dryness replacing it with freshness of life. It should be an atmosphere that is full of the life and light of the presence of God.

You have power to determine your own environment

It must be an atmosphere conducive for removing dryness and the pain that goes with it. Without creating a good atmosphere, a significant person under the spell of dryness may not survive without the word of God. Dryness in your life should be a wake up call for action. 'Dry' by definition of the Chamber's pocket dictionary means "not moist or wet, thirsty".[4] Spending quality time with dry people is one source of bringing dryness in our lives. Since the opposite of dry is moist, putting moist and dry together for long may result in cancellation of one of them.

Practice the presence of God daily

Being moist in this context is a representation of the presence of God and the anointing of the Holy Ghost. Dryness on the contrary could be a representation of the un-anointed personalities.

The anointing refreshes your life daily

In order to be conscious of the presence of God, you need to practice his presence and associate with those who love his presence and are under the anointing. Spending time with dry people will cause you to lose the moisture in your spirit.

The anointing makes you significant

The problem in our world is that many are lacking moisture; they are so dry that, they don't know or recognize the difference between moisture and dryness. You on the other hand have to grow to come to a place where you can discern an individual who is living in the anointing and an individual who lacks it and does not see the need for it. The lack of the anointing causes people to indulge into the pool of insignificance.

Psalms 42.1-3 (New American Standard Bible)

> As the deer pants for the water brooks,
>   so my soul pants for You, O God.
> My soul thirsts for God, for the living God;
>   when shall I come and appear before God?

Carry your own atmosphere

In this chapter, we are going to be looking at various issues that are associated with the season of dryness and its implications to the significant person. The first areas we will look into are examples of men in the Bible who went through the season of dryness. One pattern you will see occurring is that, these men and women

---

[4]   Chambers Pocket Dictionary and Thesaurus (UK: Chambers Harp Publishers, 2003), 189

were called by God to play a significant role in God's over all agenda for humanity in their generation.

Be determined to rise above any adversity

What does this season of dryness teach? The season of dryness teaches a significant person why leaning on God is important in winning in life. It teaches that winning in life is determined to some extend by your ability to discern the hand of God in every misfortune you face.

The grace of God attracts lots of troubles

The favour of God on your life generates unfavourable reactions by the enemy whose sole intention is to wipe you out. The enemy's' intention is to stop you by using people close to you to falsely accuse you, secondly to hate you because they are jealous of you and thirdly, they attempt to do anything to get rid of you. This is the attack we see in the life of a young man in the Bible called Joseph. His brothers hated him (Gen. 37:3-4) and this hatred led them to put him in the pit and their final decision landed him into slavery (Genesis 37.12).

Persecution is an indication of your greatness

You could be a Joseph who has probably experienced the life in the pit. You could be an individual reading this book and have experienced jealousy from some of your brothers and sisters whom you trusted and loved. One thing I want you to know is that, when God favours you, you will land into all unimaginable troubles. But all those troubles will work for you to bring you closer to what God has ordained for you to become (Romans 8.28).

The anointing makes you stand out

One of the marks of a significant person is that they attract trouble, and sometimes, they find themselves in impossible situations and yet, because God's anointing is upon their life, they come out a better person. You might have thought that Joseph would become a bitter and frustrated young man.

Challenges are for your promotion

Contrary, he became a better and a wise person due to the abuses he experienced. It has been said by Arch-Bishop Ducan Williams that "in life no matter the circumstances you face, if you do not get bitter you will get better[4]," and maintaining a spiritual perspective has a significant role to play in this respect.

The anointing is the difference maker

When you read the story of Joseph's life, you will find that, he had no problem whatsoever until his father gave him the coat of many colours (Genesis 37.3). The coat of many colours is symbolic of the anointing, thus immediately after that event, Joseph began to dream about his destiny (Gen. 37:5-11). As he could no longer keep those dreams to himself, he shared them and that is when his brothers developed hatred for him.

Your divine destiny begins when you got born again

One can observe that, Joseph dreams began after he received the coat of many colours. As a significant person, you will notice that, the same pattern can be traced in your life; you began to have dreams about what God has called you to do in this life when you became a born again child of God. You will notice that, the coming of the anointing on your life enabled you to begin to have dreams about what God has called you to do in this life (Acts 1.8).

> And it shall come to pass afterward, that I will pour out my Spirit upon all flesh; and your sons and your daughters shall prophesy, your old men shall dream dreams, your young men shall see visions: (Joel 2.28 English Standard Version)

The anointing brings overcoming power

You would think that, the coming of the anointing would result in Joseph dreams or life becoming better, but what we see is the beginning of trouble in his life. The season of dryness began immediately after the giving of the coat of many colours. What you need to know is that, the coat of many colours makes you stand out from the crowd. It makes you easy to be identified as one who has the hand of God on his life.

God is your hiding place and security

As a result, you become a target because the enemy wants to destroy you since he thinks you are a threat to him and his kingdom. But those he uses most likely to bring you down will be those most close to you.

Your vision keeps you alive

> But ye shall receive power, when the Holy Spirit is come upon you: and ye shall be my witnesses both in Jerusalem, and in all Judaea and Samaria, and unto the uttermost part of the earth (Acts 1.8 King James Version).

God's grace is sufficient for you

The persecutions in the book of Acts (Also referred to as the Acts of the Holy Spirit) did not begin before the anointing came upon the hundred and twenty who were gathered in the upper room. The troubles and hatred experienced by the early Church in the Acts of the Apostles began immediately after the anointing came upon them (Acts 4.1-4).

You have power to rise above circumstances

In the case of Joseph, the moment dryness hit his life he experienced a period of drought where the hope of experiencing the reality of his dream from a human perspective became utterly impossible. What do you do when life hits you so badly? Everything you thought about doing with your life appears impossible to accomplish? Due to a series of negative events that seem to hinder you, limit you, put you in a box and put your life on hold?

You are the one with the Holy Ghost

What do you do when all the odds are against you and for the first time in your life, you can smell it, you can feel it and can taste it? You look to the left, right and behind and all you can see is that you are defeated and your life and dreams appear to be completely shut down from a natural perspective?

Be excited about the magnitude of your challenge

What do you do when life throws all its best shots against you and ends up putting you in a pit of isolation and insecurity? Being put in a pit, Joseph must have felt helpless and insecure. What do you do when you have been wrongly treated and on top of that, you have been placed in a pit with all your hopes and dreams beside you?

The negative experience is temporary

And they took him, and cast him into a pit: and the pit was empty, there was no water in it. (Genesis 37.22)

Your situation does not look anything like your revelation

When you are in a pit, no one except you know the insecurities and fears associated with it. The feeling of loneliness and instability are burdens experienced in the pit. What a person experiences while in a pit is totally disgusting. One of the feelings this horrible experience brings is that, you find yourself in a place where darkness resides. Your new location does not allow you to see the light and hence you do not know where you are. Life is dark and gloomy.

The lower you are, the higher you will rise

The next reason is that, it makes you feel insecure because there is no life in the pit and this bring about a sense of instability. Secondly, it brings a feeling of uncertainty because you are not in control of the decisions concerning your life.

Not everyone who smiles at you likes you

The next feeling a pit experience brings is that, those whom you went to serve placed you there. It is a feeling of betrayal and abandonment. It is important to know that, you can have good intentions toward people but they might have an ulterior motive towards you.

You need to be very far-sighted

While Joseph was on his way to serve food to his brothers, they were planning about destroying him (Genesis 37.18). This incident teaches that just because you are close to a person or a group does not mean that they love or care about you. It is a good practice to always pray to God to show you the motives and intentions of those who are close to you. It helps you to conduct yourself in a manner that will not trigger feelings of jealousy and hatred in those who are not happy about your progress.

Walk with wise people

Not everyone will celebrate with you about the great future God has in store for you. God is going to link you up with the right people who will serve as an inspiration and encouragement to you. While it is a good practice to share your dreams and goals in life, it is also sensible to select cautiously those to whom you share it with. The main reason Joseph found himself in a pit was because he shared his dream with his family. They intended to destroy the young teenager who had a bright future on account of the dream he had from God.

> Even my close friend in whom I trusted, who ate my bread, has lifted up his heel against me. (Psalms 41.9)

Unveiling the pit

The pit is essentially a symbolism of limitation. Joseph's brothers placed him in a pit, as far as they were concerned, he has been limited. It is like being placed in a hole and the hole is deep to make sure that, you cannot come out and your dreams are now completed paralysed. When people put limitations on you either through action or words of hostilities, their goal is to stop you so that your dreams never become a reality. What do you do when you find yourself in that kind of situation? As for Joseph, while in a pit, the only thing he had was his dreams and the anointing.

Overcome the feeling of hopelessness

One of the feelings generated in the pit is hopelessness. In other words, the pit also signifies a hopeless situation. Joseph found himself in a hopeless situation. What do you do when you are faced with a hopeless situation? Joseph found himself in a hopeless situation as a result of his obedience to his father's instructions. Joseph did not know that obeying his father was going to cost him being put in a pit and eventually slavery and imprisonment (Genesis 37.12).

Another mystery of a pit is that, it has no name. This teaches that, when you walk with God, you can find yourself in a situation that defies all odds because you are the first to have had an experience of that degree.

God is watching over you

The next thing we can learn is that, your obedience to your father, God, does not guarantee that, you will not go through any bad experiences. Your obedience may land you into more trouble than you ever imagined. However, what you consider a trap from God's perspective is actually a safety net.

God will preserve you from trouble

A typical example is Jonah and the fish that swallowed him. From Jonah's point of view, it was the end of his life but from God's point of view, it was Jonah's salvation. This is because being in the belly of a big fish Jonah was safe from other predators in the sea (Jonah 2.23).

Obedience will cost you something

Apparently, those who obey God are the ones who experience the most persecutions. This is because Satan and his cohorts control the system of this world. Their main assignment is to abort the destiny of men and women, and when they succeed they enforce the will of Satan in that person's life.

Joseph Destiny is under attack

With regards to Joseph, the ultimate attack was targeted at aborting the plans of God in his life, but God is trillions of thousands times wiser than the devil. As far as the devil was concerned, by succeeding in placing Joseph in the pit, his dreams were going to perish with him because he had been completely limited and the location beneath the earth signifies death.

God is developing your character

Depending on how deep that pit was, no one passing by would have known Joseph was there. In fact no one expects you to be in a pit because humanity was designed to function on the surface of the earth and not beneath the earth.

The pit is an opportunity in disguise

One major characteristics of a pit is that there is no life in the pit, which is what makes it such a hopeless place to find oneself. Depending on the depth of the pit, one who is placed there may shout for help but may not be heard. As a result being in the pit generates frustration and a feeling of hopelessness. Jesus found himself in the pit of hell as well where the devil and his cohorts were trying to force him to bow to Satan but he refused and overcame them.

Colossians 2.15 (New International Version)

> And having disarmed the powers and authorities, he made a public spectacle of them, triumphing over them by the cross.

The nature of the pit is total darkness; it prevents you from seeing anything except the pit or 'your situation'. Your situation however, does not look anything like your revelation and your revelation is going to swallow up your situation like Moses snake swallowed up the Egyptian's tiny snakes (Exodus 7.8-13).

Joseph was face to face with his situation and the only way out was through Christ, the anointed in his anointing.

Lessons from the pit

The lesson we can learn from the pit experience is that, when we find ourselves in a pit, we should not let go of our dreams. It is easy to complain and become offended if those whom you trusted and looked to for guidance have mistreated you. It is easy to think about revenge if you happen to come out of that pit.

Keep walking in love always

However, you should follow the example of Joseph. You never see Joseph complaining, nor planning evil against his brothers. God was his consolation and comfort. All you need is an assurance that God is with you and he knows what you are going through in your life, and he will not leave you or forsake you. While Joseph was in the pit, God was right there with him. While his brothers were planning his elimination, God was still with him and God was also aware of what his brothers were planning to do. Since God was with him, it did not matter how deep that pit was, Joseph was lifted up from that pit.

You have what it takes to come out

This also teaches that, the fact that God is with you does not mean you will not be placed in a pit, it does not mean you will not experience troubles or what look like a hopeless situation. It just means that you will never remain in any situation you find yourself trapped in for long; you will always come out victorious.

Where you are is temporary

You could be in a pit of indecision, or you could be in a pit of confusion, a pit of stress, a pit of divorce and a pit of rejection. You could also be in a pit of insecurity and a pit of low self-esteem. However, since God is with you, meaning he is on your side, you will not remain in that problem forever. It is a season in your life and as with every season, it will soon come to an end.

> Don't be afraid, for I am with you.
> Don't be discouraged, for I am your God.
> I will strengthen you and help you.
> I will hold you up with my victorious right hand. (Isaiah 41.10 New Living Translation)

Cultivate a gratitude attitude

The next lesson that can be learned is the 'concept of silence' in the midst of mistreatment. While he was persecuted, Joseph did not speak a word against his persecutors. While he did not utter a word, it should be known that, the anointing he received was speaking. The anointing upon your life will place a restriction upon you and make you do things that are only part and parcel of the will of God upon your life.

You need to recognize the power in you

There is a group who blame God for their misfortunes and as a result, they are kept from seeing the hand of God in their lives. But those who recognize the anointing and cultivate it daily think differently from those who do not recognize the anointing.

When you receive the anointing, you become aware of so many things. Your spiritual antenna will go up and you will be awoken to the realm of God. You have the upper hand because whatever the enemy does, you will know by the anointing.

The anointing is your greatest asset

One thing you must settle in your heart is that, the devil is not afraid of you but he is scared of the anointing you have received from the Holy One. The devil wants to corrupt that anointing and if you do away with the hedge of protection, you become vulnerable. Hence, the devil wants you stressed out; he wants you to be in a state of anxiety, and God wants you to be in the exact opposite frame of mind.

> Do not be anxious about anything, but in everything, by prayer and petition, with thanksgiving, present your requests to God. (Philippians 4.6 New International Version)

The strength of your enemy is your ignorance

The enemy wants you in a place where he can play games with your mind. Satan knows that you have a dream, a dream of a brighter future. You have a strong desire to do something great with your life. As a result, he is also working behind the scenes to abort all the purposes and wonderful plans God has in store for you. Since people are the main tool he uses, you must always be on your guard against those who are negatively programmed to think and talk evil (Proverbs 8.13-14).

The Dreamer Dilemma

Genesis 37.18-20 (New International Version)

But they saw him in the distance, and before he reached them, they plotted to kill him. "Here comes that dreamer!" they said to each other. "Come now, let's kill him and throw him into one of these cisterns and say that a ferocious animal devoured him. Then we'll see what comes of his dreams.

When you have a dream, your dream will take you into places you have never imagined you will go. The greater the dream or vision you have, the greater the challenges you will have to face. Dr. Samuel Arthur once said, "Dreamers attract opposition and they are a threat to those that are pathetic and have no passion for life".[5]

God is bringing you divine connections

When you keep company with real dreamers they increase the intensity and the flames of your aspirations. They enable you to grow your vision because they are also making their vision a reality. But those without dreams will attempt to pull you down and shut you up.

Accept the help God is sending

They will try to make you feel helpless and insignificant, drain you and kill the passion in you. This is why it is important to be aware of dream killers for they are the negative people around you and you must avoid them like the plague. They will also try to talk you out of your dreams and vision.

Recognize and take advantage of divine connections

Now that you have gotten hold of this secret, you will only associate with those who are pursuing their vision in life. As a man or woman of significance, you must always become aware of the fact that, the attacks and the battles of your life are a result of the call of God upon your life.

Significant person qualities revealed

Many who found themselves in a pit were not there because they had done anything evil but rather because the devil wanted to destroy them by the medium of offense.

Reject negative words

When the enemy uses those close to you to put you down and make you feel insignificant, it is actually a sign that you are a very significant person but it is the devil way of trying to label you and negatively define you so that you can believe his lies and never aspire for anything significant.

---

[5]   Dr. Samuel Arthur, 'Message on Destiny set in stone' 2003

Don't blame God for your troubles

Secondly, when the enemy puts you in a pit, the real intention of the enemy is to cause you to blame God for your new location in life. The attitude of Joseph teaches us some quality character traits of a significant person.

A significant person like Joseph had the anointing upon his life and that anointing served as a protection, it also served as a source of strength; giving him divine insight and understanding into his situation.

You need to focus on your dreams

It did not matter where they placed Joseph because the anointing upon him was the lifting anointing and it made him have a great attitude even in the midst of his troubles. You never see Joseph weeping or feeling sorry about the situation he was placed in because he knew something that his enemies did not know. There was fundamentally something Joseph understood that his brothers did not have a clue about and that is the prophetic anointing of the Spirit.

Recognize attacks of Satan

The devil was the evil force responsible for Joseph's location from the top to the bottom of the pit. The spirit behind this attack is the spirit of jealousy, envy and murder. When you share your dreams with people close to you, they may not like you because they feel you think you are better than them and it also exposes their lack of vision and dreams. The devil incited Joseph brothers to think evil about him and when that seed was conceived and matured; it gave birth to evil actions (attempted murder).

James 1.15 (New International Version)

> Then, after desire has conceived, it gives birth to sin; and sin, when it is full-grown, gives birth to death.

Imporve the the quality of your inner circle

People are mostly comfortable around people whom they think they are superior to. There is a general class of people who are too comfortable with their present location in life. As a result, they don't want anyone surpassing them because it won't look good on them. When you are in the same living condition, they feel comfortable but as soon as you begin to make attempts to improve yourself and hence the standards of your living and quality of your life, they will try to discourage or even prevent you from taking those positive steps. That is why it is absolutely important to share your dreams with those who are doing something positive with their lives. Those who have dreams can encourage and serve as an inspiration to you.

You are a trail blazer

The devil knows that, you have a dream, and you desire to do something significant with your life. As a result, he is working behind the scenes to abort all what God has in store for you. Since humans are the only tools he uses, you must always be on your guard against those who may be attempting to talk you out of your dreams and visions through their negativism. Just because it did not work for someone does not means it won't work for you.

Talk your way up from the pit

By the anointing you have upon your life; you will turn every disappointment into appointments. You will learn to rejoice during the time of dryness. Instead of complaining, you will sing and rejoice.

> By transgression an evil man is ensnared, but the righteous sings and rejoices (Proverbs 29.6 New American Standard Bible).

You have God's approval

No matter what you go through, you will come out with a testimony if you will not let go of the word the Lord spoke to you concerning your life. If you do not give up on the prophecies made concerning your life, you will always win because of the anointing that signifies God's approval on your life.

> This command I entrust to you, Timothy, my son, in accordance with the prophecies previously made concerning you, that by them you fight the good fight, keeping faith and a good conscience, which some have rejected and suffered shipwreck in regard to their faith (1 Timothy 1.18-19 New American Standard Version)

The anointing will lift you

What or who was responsible for Joseph's removal from the pit and where did he get it from? Some may think it is Judah one of his elder brothers who felt responsible for Joseph's welfare and suggested his removal from the pit.

Genesis 37.23-28 (New International Version)

> So when Joseph came to his brothers, they stripped him of his robe – the richly ornamented robe he was wearing – and they took him and threw him into the cistern. Now the cistern was empty; there was no water in it.

> As they sat down to eat their meal, they looked up and saw a caravan of Ishmaelites coming from Gilead. Their camels were loaded with spices, balm and myrrh, and they were on their way to take them down to Egypt.

> Judah said to his brothers, "What will we gain if we kill our brother and cover up his blood? Come, let's sell him to the Ishmaelites and not lay our hands on him; after all, he is our brother, our own flesh and blood." His brothers agreed.

> So when the Midianite merchants came by, his brothers pulled Joseph up out of the cistern and sold him for twenty shekels of silver to the Ishmaelites, who took him to Egypt.

You have what it takes to persevere

The situation Joseph faced is similar to that of Jesus. When Jesus was being baptized in the Jordan and the Spirit descended upon him in the same way a dove will discern, immediately the voice came down from heaven and said 'this is my beloved Son in whom I am well pleased'. The Spirit led him in the wilderness to be tempted by the devil (Matthew 4.1 English Standard Version).

Take advantage of the power of God in you

It seems as if when the anointing came upon him, he was empowered to overcome every obstacle the devil threw at him. In the same vein, one can observe that, when Joseph was given the coat of many colours, which is symbolic of the anointing, that anointing was functioning in Joseph's life even when he was in the pit.

You are unstoppable

Due to the anointing upon his life, it did not matter where Joseph was lowered down to; the anointing was going to lift him up to where he was supposed to be. I do not know who is reading this book but I can assure you that, through the blood of Jesus Christ that was shared on the cross of Calvary for the atonement of our sins, we have received an inheritance. We have received the unction to function. The Apostle John talked about this anointing and its ability to teach us all things.

God's grace is sufficient for you

> And ye have an anointing from the Holy One, and ye know all the things (1 John 2.20 King James Version).

Because Christ is in you, your hope of glory, whatever you face, it will result in the expansion of the glory of God whose you are.

> To whom God was pleased to make known what is the riches of the glory of this mystery among the Gentiles, which is Christ in you, the hope of glory: (Colossians 1.27 American Standard Version).

You have the anointing which will cause you to rise again. You might have found yourself in a pit of stress; you are stressed out due to financial crises. The financial problem in your life is a challenge that you need to confront. The pit you find yourself in is a challenge which needs to be conquered.

Embrace your limitless power

You need to be aware that, you have what it takes to come out. Instead of complaining about your situation, instead of spending the majority of your time speaking the problem, change your attitude and change the way you talk and you will find that, it is a stepping-stone. It is all part of the process that will eventually lead you closer to your promotion. Recognize what you have within you and use it to rise above every limitation. Embrace your limitless possibilities!

See your situation as an opportunity

> As for you, you meant evil against me, but God meant it for good in order to bring about this present result, to preserve many people alive (Genesis 50.20 New American Standard Bible).

The anointing will speak

Just as the anointing on Joseph spoke when it was the appointed time for him to be lifted up from the pit, you should also keep silent and allow the processes in your life to unfold naturally at the right time. Silence means you are in total control. The anointing of God on your life will rise and make you come out of any difficult situation. No wonder the spirit of the Lord says the following, "say ye unto the righteous, it shall be well with them, for you shall eat the fruit of your labour" (Isaiah 3.10 (King James Version).

Serve God no matter what the enemy throws at you

You should note that, Joseph was not put in the pit on account of something he had done wrong; on the contrary, he was persecuted for his uprightness. Joseph was a righteous man who had a desire to serve and obey God.

The righteousness of the upright will deliver them, but the treacherous will be caught by their own greed (Proverbs 11.5 King James Version)

Like Joseph, whatever situation you find yourself, keep doing the right thing, for in consistently doing the right thing will make a way where there seems to be no way. God will cause the anointing on your life to speak on your behalf.

Right Location

The God we serve is not a dead God and as a result he knows exactly every condition in our lives and more importantly, he knows how to use what the devil intended for our burial to make it a breach into our destiny.

Your destiny is set in stone

Before time began, God had already mapped out the destiny of Joseph's life before he was born. There was nothing that happened to Joseph that was a surprise to God because he had already planned and completed Joseph's life purpose in eternity before he was born and nothing could happen in time to change the eternal counsel of God.

The destiny of Joseph was about preserving humanity in a generation where global famine had threatened to wipe out the entire human race off the face of the earth.

God always sees the bigger picture

However, Joseph who was God's man to do the job of preservation was in the wrong location. So in order to get the man of destiny at the right place, God gave him a dream (Genesis 37.5). To make it more intensive, God repeats the dream (Genesis 37.9). Now the man is possessed with the dream and as a result, he could no longer keep it to himself. He started talking about it, which created jealousy. It was jealousy and hatred that caused Joseph brothers to put him in the pit and eventually sold him into slavery.

The anointing will guide you

However from God's perspective, Joseph was on track because he was on his way to getting into the country where he was going to fulfil his destiny. However, looking at it from a natural perspective, Joseph's life was a story of disasters. His life did not make sense, because he went from one trouble to another disaster. God knew in advance that, Joseph's dream could not be fulfilled as long as he remained at his father's house.

Your season of transition is come

Can you imagine, if his brothers hated him because of his dream, how much worse do you think it would have gotten, if Joseph dream came to pass whilst living amongst his brothers? Joseph location was not conducive for his dream to become a reality.

Be ready to embrace your new location

He needed to be at a place where his dream could become a reality. He needed to be at a place where his gifts could be recognized and maximized. You can have a gift, which could be a source of provision, but because you are in the wrong location, it remains unrecognized and whatever is not recognized remains uncelebrated.

Be in the right place at the right time

Joseph needed to be at the right place where he could exercise his gift so that those around him would know what solution he contained. Being amongst his brothers however was just the wrong place because, they were not interested in helping him develop or cultivate and take advantage of the opportunities within him but they were finding a way of planning his death.

Be yourself and fully express yourself

They wanted to silence him and kill the passion God has placed in him. However, if his brothers knew that they were actually helping Joseph, they would not have done what they did to him. What appeared to be a calamity was what landed him in the right location where he realised his destiny.

The anointing assures you

As you are reading this now, the Spirit of God may be ministering to you and showing you that where ever you found yourself at this moment is not by accident or coincidence but it is a divine set up for you to meet the right person who will propel you into your destiny.

Your destiny is looking for expression

Before I formed you in the womb I knew you,
And before you were born I consecrated you;
I have appointed you a prophet to the nations" (Jeremiah 1.55 English Standard Version).

Embrace Character development

Sometimes, God will allow things to happen in your life so that you will know the people in your 'association'. God will allow things to happen so that you can see the heart of those who are close to you. God may allow things to happen so that he can use that opportunity to work on your character.

Your character is your unshakable foundation

No one comes from his or her mother's womb with a strong and well-developed character. It is the circumstances and the pressures and the demand of every day living that causes what is inside a person to get either better or get worse. So God uses the daily pressures of our lives as an opportunity to work on our character. He uses what the enemy intended for evil to bring you closer to where your gift can be recognized and celebrated. As long as Joseph remained with his brethren, Pharaoh who was the most powerful man on the planet by that time would not have known him.

God is preparing you for your purpose and destiny

The second most important thing you need to know is that, when God gives you a dream, he allows circumstances in your life in order to prepare you for that dream or vision. Being placed in the pit, Joseph learned to be content in whatever situation he found himself in and that is the attitude that is required for complete character development.

You are a supernatural being

Consider it all joy, my brethren, when you encounter various trials, knowing that the testing of your faith produces endurance (James 1.2-3 New American Standard Bible).

When you learn to refrain from arguing or complaining in whatever situation you find yourself, then you have taking a step closer to developing your character and you are also demonstrating to God through your action that you are getting ready for the next level of preparation.

> Do all things without murmurings or disputing; So that you will prove yourselves to be blameless and innocent, children of God above reproach in the midst of a crooked and perverse generation, among whom you appear as lights in the world, (Philippians 2.14 King James Version)

Pass the leadership tests

Joseph dream was for a leadership position God intended to give him but in order for Joseph to realise that dream, he needed to go through certain leadership tests to prepare him mentally, emotionally, psychologically and spiritually so that when placed in that position of influence, he would not mess up. The circumstances of his life worked to fully equip him to handle and manage what God gave him at the right time.

Embrace and maximise your season of preparation

This point also reveals that, there is a season of preparation for all purpose and vision God has given you. That is the reason God will not allow you to exercise a power that you don't know anything about. God will make sure that you go through the training and learn why you were given that gift, and you are also shown during training how the gift or that power you have been given operates. Joseph was well acquainted with the Egyptian government system and how it worked during his slavery and his time in the king's prison.

Develop stability

In other words, Joseph needed to qualify before obtaining the position God intended for him. God knows the dangers of placing a person in a leadership position that he or she has not earned or qualified for. So God planned the course to enable Joseph to go through the correct procedure and requirement to gain that leadership position.

Recognize that you are a leader

Each one of us is born with the potential of leadership but the only way we can occupy that position is when we allow God to work on us in order to develop that leadership potential in us. For some, it might take longer than others. The beginning of leadership training is when you discover what God has called you to do.

Believe in who you are

The second step is your choice of association. Sometimes like Joseph, you will not have choice of who you associate with because God has predetermined those you will be associating with to enable you to get to your destination.

From pit to slavery

Come, and let us sell him to the Ishmaelites, and let not our hand be upon him; for he is our brother and our flesh. And his brethren were content. (Genesis 37.27 New International Version)

Your testing determines your testimony

While one may think the experience of a pit is painful for Joseph, worse than being in a pit is when his brothers sold him into slavery for twenty pieces of silver. In order to understand what it meant in those days to be sold in slavery, one need to be familiar with the historical setting of that era in order to know what Joseph experienced as a slave. First and foremost, being sold to the Ishmaelites and taken to Egypt was for Joseph a totally new environment.

The bigger the challenge the greater the testimony

The language of the Egyptians was a barrier to him; hence he needed to learn the language. As a slave, he had no rights and as a result, he was under the control of his master. Joseph was about to start a new life all over again in a foreign land as a slave. He needed to put up with lots of external challenges: language barrier, cultural barrier, social barrier, and religious barrier.

Hold unto your dreams during times of uncertainty

As a slave since he could only do as his master commanded him, he had no choice but to do as he was told. Now being a slave in Egypt is a terrible experience because the Egyptians treatment of their slaves was unpleasant. As a slave, he had no privileges or future.

You have to know who you are in order to overcome

To be a slave in that land meant you had absolutely no life of your own. Your master owned you and he did to you as he pleased. Your master would decide your fate and you did not have any control over what was going to happen to you in the future. Whatever gods your master worshipped automatically became the god you were supposed to serve. When you analysed what went on daily in a slave's life, you will realise that, Joseph was facing serious and embarrassing challenges.

Fight the good fight of faith

How do you feel if you realised that your life is no more yours and some one else is deciding what your purpose in life should be? What do you do when you are in a situation where you feel like everything is working against you though you have a great dream to do something significant with your life?

Refuse to give up during opposition

What do you do when God has given you a dream but you find yourself doing something that you feel is insignificant and have nothing to do with your life purpose? Have you ever been in a situation where you feel like you are being exploited, controlled, used, and manipulated? How does that make you feel? It makes you feel helpless and hopeless. It makes life appear meaningless and purposeless. What do you do after you come out of a terrible crisis, you think everything is now over but all of a sudden, you land in a major problem which defies all odds? Joseph did not have any hope as far as his status was concerned. The only thing he had was God and the anointing which was infused in him through the coat of many colours.

Refuse to compromise your dignity

As you are reading, you may identify with Joseph's situation one way or the other. You might not own anything as yet in the natural. You might be in a situation where you don't have a life of your own because other things society considers important have taking all the spaces in your life: government, legal, technology, institutions, organizations and family responsibilities.

Don't be a slave to society definitions

You feel like, society owns you because your very existence has been fully occupied by responsibilities given to you by society, and you feel trapped and unable to get out of the system created by society. In fact society compels you to take on more responsibilities that society has not prepared you for. Society says for instance, get a job or get a house but you have no clue as to how to get any of these functions.

God is your source, not society and its government

The present system is set up in such a way that only a few fortunate people are benefiting from it due to some great connections. Have you ever heard the saying, "It is not what you know but who you know that makes a difference in your life?" The present system is set up in such a way that you feel like you have no chance of owning anything worthwhile.

If your life is viewed from a logical standpoint, your life does not make sense because it consists of a bunch of messes because everything you ever worked for is for the enhancement and betterment of the life of those whom you work for. If that is the condition of your situation, you can be assured that, it is only temporary.

You are born for the triumphant life in Christ

Always remember that, everything you are going through is subject to change if you will not allow the devil to steal your dreams. What ever you are under right now you are going to be over soon. Whatever is ruling you now, you are going to be ruling very soon. Somebody somewhere will one day need to hear your testimony to come out of his or her mess. Your testing determines your testimony and your mess determines your message. As your mess becomes your message, it will be of benefit to someone.

Faith always prevails

You will observe that, life throws challenges that sometimes defy logical explanation. But when you look at those challenges with God's eye (eye of faith) you begin to smile even in the midst of your staggering situation.

When you find out that, behind those impossible situations there is God who is aware of what you are going through, you will begin to enquire of him about your problem and unfair treatments.

Recognize the enemy of your destiny

God wants to teach you that, beyond that unfair treatment is an adversary who hates you because of the anointing which produces the favour of God upon your life. God may be helping you to understand that, though the enemy is fighting you through people, his real intention is to distract you from seeing things the way they really are.

Maintain your position in the midst of oppositions

He will attempt to confuse you if you allow him because his intentions are to keep you unaware of the invisible battle over your destiny. The devil lost his destiny and as a result, he does not want any one fulfilling their destiny. Your destiny is to save someone but the enemy is jealous and anxious and wants to destroy you before you get to that person or nation.

Since we are vulnerable while young, he attempts to destroy many either through evil words spoken and aimed at you or through physical attempts made by those close to you to destroy you knowingly or unknowingly.

Look beyond your present circmustances

The bottom line is if you knew exactly what was happening in the realm of the spirit, you would develop a different attitude about your entire existence.

The enemy is not seen in the physical realm but those who have given access to him through avenues of envy, jealousy and wickedness; he can use them as a tool in this natural realm to carry out his agenda and evil intentions towards you.

Use your discernment to see through your enemy

What do you think the devil and his cohorts are planning and scheming against you? The best question should be: What are you doing as one with a destiny to bless your generation, to counter and defend yourself against the purposes of the devil? The wiles of the devil are the strategies which are the deceptions of the enemy and that is all the ammunition the devil has because he has been completely paralysed and defeated by Jesus Christ.

You are superior to Satan

Are you just sitting there or are you standing and taking your ground like a soldier in fierce battle over your destiny? Dr. Myles Munroe in his inspirational book states the following, "Destiny demands diligence" and he also states "Persistence is the desire to withstand every opposition"[6]

Cultivate the winning attitude

This is the attitude that should be adopted by those who want to fulfil their destiny. You must be willing to identify the enemies to your destiny. However before that you need to understand that your destiny is not in the hand of any human being. But human beings will play a part in either enabling you to understand your destiny or they may attempt to stop you because they are under the spell of the devil.

---

[6] Myles Munroe, The principle and the power of vision (Whitaker House: USA, 2003), 203

Your favour determines your warfare

The story of David and the hatred he experienced by king Saul is a typical example of how the victory or destiny of one person can easily intimidate another who has insecurities. David's victory over Goliath who was Israel's' most notorious enemy ended up generating hatred for David.

The size of your problem determines the size of your reward

When King Saul felt like David was receiving more national recognition than him, he became jealous. As a consequence of his victory, David became the most wanted enemy of King Saul in Israel. He attempted many times to destroy the young man for no apparent reason except that; he has killed the most notorious enemy of Israel. David's narrative teaches every significant individual reading this book a vital lesson about why some people close to you can be planning your downfall all because of the favour of God upon your life.

Keys to Surviving Hardship

When Joseph was sold to Potiphar as a slave his attitude teaches us some important lessons about the kind of attitude we should have in times of unfair treatment. One of the reasons Joseph had a great attitude or superior attitude was because his dream was more real to him and that kept him focused.

Have a clear focus

Joseph had the right focus about his existence. The principle governing focus is that when you focus on something, you create the necessary condition to produce or create what you have been focusing on. In other words when you focus on something, you attract it into your life. That is why, focusing on your dreams, by thinking about them and talking about them everyday is a major factor in making it a reality.

One reason many fail in life is because they focus on many things instead of focusing on the one most important thing that they can do well in. The key to becoming an expert in an area is you must become hundred percent committed to that thing until it becomes a reality. Commitment is the foundation and catalyst for change.

Nothing before the time but God's timing is the best

The next lesson about Joseph attitude is that you do not need to be on the mountain top to be happy. The happiness of Joseph is not because of persecutions but happiness and peace in spite of the circumstances around him. We can tell that

Joseph was displaying happiness because Potiphar saw something about Joseph that led him to put him in charge of his household and servants.

The bigger the problem, the bigger the anointing

While a slave, he demonstrated the spirit of responsibility and the spirit of leadership. He did not seem to see or think of himself as a slave because he knew his background as one who was from a renowned family.

Joseph simply acted out what he thought he was. Unlike Joseph, many people do the opposite. When they find themselves in a trying situation and that situation has labelled them, they accept that stigma and begin to act as though that was their new identity. Circumstances can easily define you and confine you if you allow them.

See youself as God sees you

The Bible says, "For as he thinks within himself, so he is. He says to you, "Eat and drink!" But his heart is not with you (New American Standard Bible). This verse of scripture teaches a very powerful principle which many of us are not aware of. When your present condition defines you, places a limit on you physically or mentally, do you accept that definition? The status of Joseph was that of a slave but his attitude, the way he thought of himself, the manner in which he carried himself teaches otherwise. His behaviour and actions were a result of the information he held within himself.

Think and act like a king

When Potiphar saw the way Joseph conducted himself, he treat him differently from the rests of his slaves. This is because the way you see yourself (self image) reflects in your behaviour and attitude. As a result of what people see, they treat you accordingly. Without saying a word, you are sending or revealing a lot of private information you hold within yourself through your behaviour, and people are more concerned about your behaviour than anything else.

Your thoughts create your inner belief system and your beliefs determine your values, which determines your mindset and your mindset determines your destiny.

Our physical universe is made of limitless possibilities

Whatever people have done to you, whatever status you have now because of maltreatment, whatever label people have given you, don't see it as a permanent condition. Don't accept what people have called you due to your present condition as your ultimate reality. It is important to find out what God thinks of you instead of others opinion about you. Think of yourself in terms of the dreams God has given you and the desires he has placed in your heart.

Keep dreaming big

While the narrator of the life of Joseph is silent about Joseph's reaction to the persecutions he experienced, by careful examination one can tell from the outcome of his life that he was optimistic, he maintained a superior attitude. His response was positive probably because he was aware of his covenant with God through Abraham and his grand-father Isaac. Another major factor could be that, he knew that his dream would surely come to pass and God might have been assuring him about his purpose.

What you see is not all there is

Those key points are important because it helped Joseph look at his life from God's perspective (Faith). If he looked at his life from a natural perspective, all he could see is a life that was meaningless and purposeless. A life that was marked by perpetual trouble was the sum total of Joseph's life. But the favour of God upon Joseph's life made the persecutions bearable. It made him maintain a positive attitude during his time of dryness.

Know Your God

The second key to surviving in your times of dryness is that, you have to know the God you are serving. There are many who claim to know God but are deceiving themselves. There are others, who serve the gods of their father or grandfather like Joseph did, but the true is, you need to know whom you are serving. Jesus said unto the Samaritan woman" You Samaritans know very little about the one you worship, while we Jews know all about him, for salvation comes through the Jews." (John 4.22, New Living translation).

Transition from religion to relationship

So many do not know the God they are serving because they are following in the traditions of their parents and grandparents. However, that can be a problem, because if you just follow without making any enquiry about the god they served, you could be serving a dead god.

Pursue intimacy with the Father

There are so many religions in the world but religion can only point out your need for a relationship with God but it does not give you the relationship you are seeking. According to Dr. Myles Munroe, "religion is man in search for God", but in Christianity, you are given the opportunity to enter into a relationship with God[7].

Result of intimacy is sychronization

That is why the second key to surviving hardship teaches you to learn how to develop friendship with your creator through spending quality time with him so that you can be aware of his presence at all times in your life.

God is willing to solve any problems you are dealing with

The result of God's anointing in your life is that you can overcome any obstacle that comes your way. Since the God of Abraham, Isaac and Jacob is the person who is the only specialist in solving impossible situations, if you know him, whatever difficulty you face in life will be an opportunity for him to prove himself strong on your behalf.

Get to know God as your friend

But if you do not know him, you will not expect him to act on your behalf. This is what the nature of covenant teaches; God loves everybody but he is only responsible for those who have accepted Jesus Christ as their Lord and Saviour. He is only responsible to those who are his children, the seed of Abraham.

Allow God to train you in the things of the Spirit

However, being in a relationship with God also means you are responsible for carrying out God's instructions on this planet earth. One important point you must absolutely settle in your heart is the fact that, you cannot survive your season of dryness if you do not know God. God will not allow you to go through certain experiences if he knows that you don't have the relationship level you need to have with God in order to go through that experience. God allowed Joseph to go through that experience of being a slave because he knew that Joseph has a relationship with the Father to enable him to go through and come out stronger than he went in. It basically comes down to what you have seen, because what God has shown you will determine the experiences required to enable you get to that destination. God will only give you what you can handle and not what you ask for.

---

[7]   Dr. Myles Munroe, Rediscovering The Kingdom (Bahamas: Destiny Image publishers, 2004), 36

God desires a deeper fellowship with you

In order for Joseph to survive the experience of being a slave, he needed to know God because his knowledge (awareness) of God enabled him to maintain a great attitude in the house of Potiphar despite the challenges he had to face due to his low status.

God is taking you to a new level in Him

If you were like Joseph who had a dream of becoming a ruler but you found yourself being sold in slavery, what kind of thinking would you have adopted? If you were like Joseph, you would have probably thought of yourself in terms of what God has shown you instead of allowing your present circumstances to define who you are.

... And such as do wickedly against the covenant shall he corrupt by flatteries: but the people that do know their God shall be strong and do exploits. (Daniel 11.32 King James Version)

Respond Positively

Even in your darkest moments, you must reject all negativism

The third key then to surviving hardship is your decision to respond positively in the midst of bad treatment. Your bad treatment should remind you that you do not belong at your present location. It is an indication that where you are cannot define you because it is a temporary location. That is only made possible if you know God and are sure of the dream God has given you.

Have the self-discipline to maintain a positive outlook

In the midst of bad treatment, what keeps you being a better person is your knowledge (revelation knowledge) that God cannot lie hence you believe that your situation is subject to change. Due to the bright future Joseph envisioned, he could afford to experience a temporary setback.

Your future is greater than your past

According to the writer of Hebrews, because of the joy that was set before him (Jesus Christ) he could afford to go through the shame of the cross because he knew that it was a temporary set back, therefore, he ignored the embarrassment and shame (Hebrews12.2).

God will give to you double for your trouble

Why do many people become bitter instead of getting better during a trying situation? The reason lots of people who have been called to greatness become average are their lack of knowledge (revelation knowledge) of the reasons behind their troubles. Understanding why things are the way they are in your life helps you develop a positive attitude.

Your enemies are as necessary as your friends

Having a positive attitude in a trying situation is only possible if you know that behind the troubles you are presently dealing with is the throne. With that revealed knowledge, your response to persecution will be optimistic.

This explains why Jesus said, "Blessed are you when men shall persecute you and say all manner of evil against you for my sake, rejoice and be exceedingly glad, for great is your reward in heaven." In other words, the reason for your persecution is because of the greatness you are carrying. Always remember that, the greater the trouble you have to endure, the greater the personal development.

Upward and forward only that is your life

Your progress in life is your willingness to endure every opposition against your dreams and still maintain a superior attitude. When you do this, you are demonstrating a certain level of emotional maturity and emotional stability and these are quality character traits of every successful leader.

Your path is like a shining light

It also reveals that, the circumstances needed in your life to enable you to develop emotional maturity are troubles and persecutions. When Joseph was at Potiphar's house, he did not have a choice as a slave; he did not have any rights either. It was a rough life because he had to do what he was commanded. He could not complain because as a slave, your master does to you as he pleases. As a result of these limitations, he was forced to develop emotionally. God knew that in order to develop emotional maturity and stability, Joseph needed a certain degree of social and cultural condition to enable him to become exactly what he wanted him to become.

God is getting ready to release you into your destiny

As you are reading this, you might have been placed in a situation that you feel is a degrading condition. Though you have a dream, your present circumstances have limited you and given you a poor status. However, what you do not know is God could be using those troubles to your advantage. God is using it to develop emotional maturity and stability in you. This is because where God is about to place you demand a great responsibility, which requires a certain level of emotional and psychological maturity and psychological independence. God is aware that without those fundamental qualities, you will not be prepared to face the challenges associated with that leadership position God wants you to occupy.

God is bringing you into maturity

A person who is emotionally matured and stable is not controlled by external conditions; he is not moved by the appearance but the content. This is an important leadership trait because; a leader is looked to for direction and solutions in times of crises.

Emotional fortitude is desirable

As a result, he or she has not got the time to be emotionally controlled by the way things appear to be. Since God was preparing Joseph to be a ruler in the Egyptian empire, God needed to allow a problem in the life of Joseph in order to develop him emotionally and make him stable. As far as God was concerned, the season of slavery in Joseph's life was an important moment for Joseph's personal development. You could be in a situation similar to Joseph, and you do not know why your life is full of trouble but God may be using this book to teach you that he is preparing you for a great leadership position.

Reasons for era of dryness

When Joseph was at Potiphar's house, he learned lots of lessons about servant leadership. As a servant in his master's house, he learnt the importance of treating his master and all those who were under him with respect. As one who was the head of the servants, he learned to treat every one fairly and equally.

The spirit of humility is growing in you

The spirit of humility, which is cultivated by great leaders, was also an opportunity for Joseph to grow in humbleness. God knew that this was the way for Joseph to develop into the kind of leader he wanted him to become. If Joseph remained with his father and brothers, he would not have had the right circumstances to enable God to teach him the wisdom to lead nations in times of global famine. It is worth noting then that the wisdom required in ruling an Empire is a unique kind of wisdom that can only come through certain circumstances. Without the season of slavery,

Joseph would probably remain average and obscure leader. The circumstances of his life are what developed Joseph into a great leader in Egyptian Empire.

Avoid premature exposure in leadership

The narrative of Joseph's life reveals the dangers of attempting to run away from where God has presently placed you. You have to understand that God has placed you where you are at the moment for a season and for a reason. God wants to teach you some secrets about life that you cannot gain anywhere else except through that negative experience of life. By attempting to get away because you feel uncomfortable, you are rejecting a fundamental training programme which could sabotage what God intends to do in your life.

Endure hardship as a good soldier

By getting away, you expose yourself to danger because you are not in the will of God concerning your life. Being out of the purpose of God could cripple you and render you utterly useless, because you begin to operate on your own initiative instead of the wisdom of God. In these verses (Acts 21.1-5) and (Acts 21.10) you will discover some useful insights about the importance of allowing the will of God to be done.

Effectively handling your situation

The third key to surviving hardship is your decision to focus on your dream instead of your situation. Many people fail in life because what they are focusing on is the wrong thing. It is very easy to see your situation as your ultimate reality or your top priority. It is very easy to allow yourself to be overwhelmed by the impossible situations you find yourself in.

Learn to encourage yourself in the Lord

The reason you are so angry is probably because you were not the cause of it, like Joseph those close to you could be the source of your troubles. As a result, it is easy to sit down and feel sorry for yourself and complain about everything that is wrong with you instead of handling it effectively.

Accept the wisdom of God

The wisdom of God will tell you to change your focus, because what you are doing to yourself is causing more harm than good. The wisdom of God will inform you about the disadvantages and advantages of focus; eventually, what you focus on will control the outcome of your life.

Your situation is a stepping stone

When you focus on the problem, you will not think about the solution. That is why it is so important to know what you are focusing on in times of dryness. For example, a person who is sick should not focus on the disease but should focus on the promises of God on health and wellness. In the midst of your situation, by focusing on your dreams, your situation will be seen differently. As you focus on your vision of a better future, you will begin to see the situation as a stepping-stone to your destiny. Whatever you are facing now is meant to bring you closer to your destination. Your troubles like Joseph are access points to your destiny. Put your imagination to work and create the future you want by the power of visualization. See yourself already occupying that position that God has shown you.

What you focus on multiplies

Focus should be perceived or identified in a significant person's life as a major factor in making your dream become a tangible reality. What sustain your focus are your beliefs and what strengthens your believing is your willingness to keep hearing and seeing your dream. You need to believe that your dream will become a reality. Make it a habit to declare who you are, and declare your dreams and vision daily.

Keep your dreams on the tablet of your heart

Let your dream become your only obsession in life. By declaring what you believe, you are creating an inner image, which will keep getting bigger until people begin to see it in you. As your dream becomes bigger in you, your priorities also change, your dream will begin to dictate how you live your life. While Joseph was in his master's house, he lived there with other slaves but he did not live like them because, his priority was his vision and since his focus was on where he was going, he did not allow his present circumstances as a slave to distract him. Joseph believes were translated into faith – he perceived himself and carried himself as a Prince.

Commitment is essential for fulfilment of your vision

The secret to Joseph's success in Egypt is the power of focus. When you observe people who accomplish great things for God, you will see the supernatural power of focus at work in their lives. Some of these great women and men of God did great exploits because they had a vision from God and committed their lives to pursuing it with all their heart. In spite of impossible situations that came their way to try to stop them, they maintained their focus. The devil is after your dreams; he is after your focus as well, because he knows that, when he can succeed in controling your focus, he can succeed in destroying your dreams. Remember that, it is your vision that fuels your passion and your vision keeps you alive.

Make this principle work for you

Now that you know the importance of focus how are you going to make it work for you? First, you can make it an advantage by prioritizing your life. What immediate thing are you attempting to accomplish with your life right now? There are some immediate, menial things like your education, your goals of becoming a healthier person etc. What are you doing in order to make yourself the best in the area of your expertees? Since your education is the road map to your destiny, your focus should be on improving yourself so that you can enrich your personality.

Display your efficiency at work or in your business

As Joseph was placed in the Egyptian house, you might have been placed in that company to bring a change through the power of focus. When Joseph was in the house of slavery, he focused on how best he could serve his master. By putting the power of focus at work, he was able to manage Potiphar house effectively. One of the reasons Joseph received recognition was because he put the power of focus at work in his life.

Summary

The aspect of this chapter was addressing the keys to surviving hardship in your time of dryness.

To summarise, the first and the most important key was attitude. The most important characteristic with people with superior attitude is that they are in charge of their emotions inspite of what life is throwing at them. They do not allow their emotions to control how they respond to bad treatments. Instead of reacting to what some one has done to them, they respond in a mature way, they respond in wisdom and in the love of God because love is the driving force of their lives.

Depend on God to fulfil your destiny

The second principle to surviving hardship was your intimate relationship with God. It was observed that, a person with a solid relationship with God lives in the realm of the supernatural. As a result, what is happening around them can only make them stronger, better and not bitter. A person's who know God knows everything because God tells them how to deal wisely in the affairs of their life (Joshua 1.8).

The third principle to surviving hardship is the supernatural power of focus. When you are focus on your dreams, you create the necessary condition to make it a tangible reality.

Potiphar's wife bad Attitude

Genesis 39.7-10 (New International Version)

> And after a while his master's wife took notice of Joseph and said, "Come
> to bed with me!"

> But he refused. "With me in charge," he told her, "my master does not
> concern himself with anything in the house; everything he owns he has
> entrusted to my care. No one is greater in this house than I am. My master
> has withheld nothing from me except you, because you are his wife. How
> then could I do such a wicked thing and sin against God?" And though
> she spoke to Joseph day after day, he refused to go to bed with her or
> even be with her.

The next aspect that is of relevance to the subject of the era of dryness as
shown in Joseph's life is the bad attitude of Potiphar wife towards Joseph. The wife
of Potiphar is a representation of the Jezebel spirit. This is a principality in charge
of control, manipulation and sexual sin.

Identifying Jezebel

In this part of the Bible, Jezebel was unknown, it was the first time it introduced
itself through Potiphar's wife. The fact that Potiphar's wife's name was not mentioned
should tell you something. It says that Jezebel has many ways in which it manifests
itself hence the name Jezebel is inadequate to fully grasp the understanding of the
Jezebel spirit. The spirit of Jezebel is ultimately the devil incarnate.

Be strong in the Lord and his power

While Joseph was minding his own business (focused on what his master put
him in charge of), the spirit of control, manipulation and sexual sin was jealous and
wanted to distract him from his assignment because she wanted some attention, as
Joseph was receiving most of the attention from her husband.

Take advantage of the strength of God in you

Genesis 39.11-12 (New International Version)

One day he went into the house to attend to his duties, and none of the household
servants was inside. She caught him by his cloak and said, "Come to bed with me!"
But he left his cloak in her hand and ran out of the house.

The command to Joseph was "Come to bed with me"! What made this woman react this way is unknown but one thing that is clear is that, she was compelled by a power that overtook her. However, when Joseph refused, another aspect of Jezebel was revealed, and that is force and intimidation. She held Joseph's coat and while Joseph ran the coat was left in her hand.

Sin shall not have dominion over you

Genesis 39.13-15 (New International Version)

When she saw that he had left his cloak in her hand and had run out of the house, she called her household servants. "Look," she said to them, "this Hebrew has been brought to us to make sport of us! He came in here to sleep with me, but I screamed. When he heard me scream for help, he left his cloak beside me and ran out of the house."

Another aspect of Jezebel was revealed when she used that as evidence in accusing Joseph for sexual harassment. The real intention of the spirit of Jezebel operating in this woman was revealed when Joseph refused her sexual advances. The position Joseph held in her husband's house was something that she detested. However in order to find a point of accusation, she needed evidence.

Joseph Character is tested

This narration reveals Joseph's character. What kind of person was Joseph after all those negative experiences? There are other lessons that you and I can learn to abide by while in our era of dryness. One important thing you should be aware of is that, the devil is the personality behind these horrific attacks.

You have authority by the anointing

By making herself available, the devil used her in order to bring Joseph down from the position he held in her husband's house. This is a classic example of a place in the Bible where the devil attempted to steal a person position through sexual temptation. Like we said earlier on, in order to get you out of your position, he will need a vessel that he can use. One of the most effective weapons the devil uses against people of significance is their desire for instant gratification. What is the basis for temptation? The basis for temptation is hunger.

Refuse to allow Satan to use you

The narrator does tell us the many attempts she repeatedly made day in and day out in order to come to a point where she literally wanted to force Joseph into the idea of sleeping with her. How many great men and women have forfeited their destiny all because of one foolish action? How many great men have destroyed their reputation because of sexual temptation? In your time of dryness, this is one of the temptations to watch out for. Promiscuous women and men are everywhere but you should not be one of those who give them access in your life.

Remain in your position of power

They come to you using ingenious tactics and try to seduce you into sexual sin. However, you must be aware that behind that beautiful woman or man could be a Jezebel spirit who is responsible for every sexual temptation and every sexual sin.

You are a target of Satan

This spirit targets those who have a great destiny to fulfil. Its sole intent is to stop your vision or dream before it becomes a reality. It is like when you kill a baby, you have prevented a full-grown man or woman from being revealed in this baby. This spirit tries to short-circuit what God has intended to accomplish with your life. Always remember that whatever God has planned for you will only become a reality based on your level of cooperation with his leading and direction.

Recognize and conquer Jezebel

How do you identify a Jezebel spirit and when can you discern that you are making an unholy alliance with the spirit of Jezebel? When someone wants to use you to do something contrary to your convictions and your God given destiny, it is a controlling and manipulative spirit. While this spirit is known for sexual sins, it can also use men and women as well to manipulate and control others using intimidation.

Refuse to bow to Jezebel tactics

Genesis 39.17-20 (New International Version)

> She kept his cloak beside her until his master came home. Then she told him this story: "That Hebrew slave you brought us came to me to make sport of me. But as soon as I screamed for help, he left his cloak beside me and ran out of the house."

> When his master heard the story his wife told him, saying, "This is how your slave treated me," he burned with anger. Joseph's master took him and put him in prison, the place where the king's prisoners were confined.

This spirit will attempt to twist your words and make you appear as a bad person, for the main aim of this spirit is to destroy your reputation. It really becomes difficult to avoid the influence of this spirit if you are living in the same house. How are Jezebels created and come into a house, organization or communities? It is when real men are reluctant to take their place in their home or society, thus the spirit of Jezebel shows up to take charge of situations.

Refusing to Compromise

When you associate with the wrong people, they will attempt to make you think like them and talk like them. You must keep away from wicked people; make sure you don't spend quality time with them because their negative influence will affect you. When you choose your friends carefully, you keep yourself from trouble, which comes to those who associate with bad company.

Genesis 39.10 (New International Version)

> And though she spoke to Joseph day after day, he refused to go to bed with her or even be with her.

Overcome the Test of Character

Gen. 39:6-7 (New International Version)

> So he left in Joseph's care everything he had; with Joseph in charge, he did not concern himself with anything except the food he ate.

> Now Joseph was well-built and handsome, and after a while his master's wife took notice of Joseph and said, "Come to bed with me!"

The test of character reveals what you are made of and this sexual temptation faced by Joseph, and his decision to run away from it reveals Jospeh character. Good character then is when you have an opportunity to do the wrong thing but you refuse to do it fearing no consequences of your right action. A person without character would have easily fallen for that sexual temptation because he would have seen it as an opportunity to prove that his status in his boss house is not as a slave but as the head.

Cultivate and maintain a good character

However a person with a good strong character will not allow themselves to be reduced to the desires and needs of anybody. While Joseph might have gotten away with sleeping with his master's wife, he would have shown to God that he is unqualified for the position God was about to entrust in his care in Egypt.

Refuse to yield to pressures of your society

Genesis 39.19-20 (New International Version)

When his master heard the story his wife told him, saying, "This is how your slave treated me," he burned with anger. Joseph's master took him and put him in prison, the place where the king's prisoners were confined.

But this incidence also reveals the mark of an individual who knew he was going somewhere; he had no time for any little foolishness, which had the potential to sabotage his destiny. Joseph refusal to partake of the immoral conduct of the land of Egypt led to his imprisonment. When you choose to do the right thing, you will face persecutions. When you choose to do the right thing, the devil will hate you for it because he is the father of wickedness.

Never give any opportunity to Satan

As a result by refusing to do the wrong thing, Satan has lost an opportunity to steal from you. On the other hand, by doing the right thing, you have shown to God that his way is right and God will add to you honour, greatness, beauty, and spiritual growth. You might not feel it but something good is always added to you when you choose to do the right thing all the time. When you consistently do what God says to do, you are in reality setting yourself up for promotion.

Genesis 39.21-23 (New International Version)

But while Joseph was there in the prison, the Lord was with him; he showed him kindness and granted him favor in the eyes of the prison warden. So the warden put Joseph in charge of all those held in the prison, and he was made responsible for all that was done there. The warden paid no attention to anything under Joseph's care, because the Lord was with Joseph and gave him success in whatever he did.

You need to qualify for promotion and rulership

On the other hand, doing the wrong thing is equally a set up for inheriting demotion and shame. Satan will present to you many opportunities to fall but you must be aware that the consequences for choosing to do the wrong thing will only bring you pain and demotion. In a society that promotes immoral behaviour, doing the right thing can be difficult, especially when you are a Christian. Since Joseph was chosen to be a star in Egypt, he needed to prove to God that he was worthy of the position God was about to entrust him with.

Your promotion is based on choosing good over evil

By running from the sexual advances of his master wife, he demonstrated to God that he would do the right thing even if it will cost him being put in prison. This point is crucial because God will not promote you if you willingly choose evil over good. If you get involved in any immoral behaviour, you are disqualifying yourself and delaying your rightful position in the Lord. A person who is still doing what God is passionately against is unqualified for a leadership position in the house of God.

Proverbs 3.7-8 (New International Version)

> Do not be wise in your own eyes; fear the Lord and shun evil. This will
> bring health to your body and nourishment to your bones

Follow after examples of good people

There are so many people in the church who are delaying their promotion due to bad character. You must be willing to demonstrate to God that you are ready to be promoted. Promotion and progress comes to those who are seeking it earnestly through seeking the direction of God for their life. Each time you are promoted, more anointing is increased in your life. The result of choosing to do the right thing is character development. The result of treating someone right who treated you bad gives you an upper hand over him or her. Your action shows that, you are not at their level morally and spiritually and the result is promotion and honour.

Understanding intimidation

The word "intimidation" is defined by Chambers Pocket Dictionary and thesaurus as follows: "to frighten or threaten into submission"[8] What does this meaning of intimidation teach about Joseph's encounter with Potiphar's wife? It teaches that the spirit of Jezebel can manifest as a spirit of intimidation and the sole intent of this spirit is to control your life through fear.

---

[8] Chambers Pocket Dictionary and Thesaurus (Edinburgh: Chambers Harrap Publishers, 20003), 332

Genesis 39.7

Now Joseph was well-built and handsome, and after a while his master's wife took notice of Joseph and said, "Come to bed with me!"

Be strong and courageous

When you are in the presence of an intimidating spirit, you will recognize the following: that the individual lacks self-esteem and in order to feel like they are in control, they do or say something because they know that they have a certain degree of authority over you: they attempt to use their position to make you submit to them forcefully. This is what you need to watch out for. For people or anybody who attempts to use fear to make you do something you don't want to do. The major lesson Joseph's action teaches is that, just because someone is feeding you and doing everything for you does not give them permission to use intimidation to control you. They might own your time but they are not the owner of your soul.

Reasons for intimidation

When someone intimidates you, in their thinking, they see you as a victim. A victim is a person who is under the control of another. Another vital reason someone may intimidate you is because they don't like you and in order to get rid of you or display their hatred, they use threats to push you away.

God has made you a king and a priest

Mostly, the relationship between master and slave is an environment where you see the spirit of intimidation functioning at its highest peak. Since a slave is subject to his master, the – master if he is wicked – will use his authority as a tool to intimidate his subjects. Ultimately, the use of authority to intimidate is actually an abuse of authority. Because the master of a slave knows that he owns them, his approach of ruling is very authoritarian and tyrannical.

You are a master over your environment

A tyrannical ruler will say, "You must do what I instruct else you will bear the consequences of your disobedience." As a significant person, you might have been in a situation where someone uses his or her position of authority to abuse you through intimidation. Why do I label it as an abuse? Because when someone does not know the purpose of their position, they abuse it. Dr. Myles Munroe puts it well; he says, "When purpose is unknown, abuse is inevitable"[9] People who lack knowledge about the purpose for authority end up abusing their authority. An abuser of authority is an individual who feel worthless and suffers from low self-esteem, but in order to make themselves feel like they are somebody, they use their position of influence to bring their subjects down through lies and verbal abuses.

You have the power within to recover

If you are someone who has been affected by the spirit of intimidation you might feel like you are not in control of your life and as a result, you end up treating yourself like you are nothing. You might even begin to think that you are a mistake and as a result, you accept anything that comes your way because you have no sense of standard in your life. Let me warn you, if you have no standards in your life you are not ready for any kind of relationship in the social market place.

Maintain a high standard at all times

A person without a standard is a person who needs healing in their life. My advice to you is to seek professional help, speak to your clergy about it. You need to seek wholeness in your spirit, soul and body. People will walk all over you because you allow them to due to your low self-esteem. In order to develop any form of relationship, you need to spend time with God so that he can help you to develop a proper relationship with yourself.

Recognize and celebrate your true value

Lack of knowledge of your true value will result in people attempting to define you, and devalue you. If you have not developed a proper friendship with yourself, because you are your first best friend, you will begin to accept those stigmas, which will in turn make you more insecure and set you up for more failures in your future relationships.

An example of high standard

If you want to meet a person who had a high standard for their life, I am happy to present to you Joseph. Joseph reminds me of someone who knew what was more important in life and how to guard it against pollution. How do we know this? By

---

9   Myles Munroe, I n Pursuit of Purpose (Bahamas: Destiny image Publishers: 1992) 39

reading the account of the interaction between Joseph and his master's wife, I can tell that, Joseph was a man of standards. Joseph would not compromise and tarnish his name by sleeping with his master's wife (Genesis 39.9-10).

Principle of integrity revealed

He refused to destroy his reputation and the reputation of his God. If he compromised, he would have shown by his action that, he was a man who lacks integrity. Integrity is dealing honestly and truthfully no matter where you find yourself. It would have undermined his position with God as well because he would have communicated through his action his lack of trust in his God to give him a wife if he needed one at that moment in his life. Take five minutes to think about your life. What are you communicating to God through your actions?

Action does speak louder than words

There are many of us who are communicating lack of trust in God's ability to give us a wife or a husband who will truly play the role she or he was meant to play. There are others who are communicating indirectly to God that he is not needed. As a result such people live their life in darkness (recklessly) because ignoring God is equal to ignoring light and the consequences of ignoring where light can be found is walking in a path where it is dark.

Maintain your ground

Refuse to step out of righteousness, as Kenneth Copeland perfectly puts it "doing what is right only for one reason because it is right and you do it right the first time,"[5] as an act of righteousness. With this kind of approach to life, you will never make mistakes that will delay your promotion. That is why the Apostle John says, "when you walk in the light as he is in the light, there is no occasion of stumbling." (1John 1.7) Stepping in darkness is dangerous because you don't see where you are going. But by reading Joseph's response and reaction to temptation, we should also learn to do the right thing. Doing the right thing is the only way to walk with God and in order to fulfil our destiny; we need to learn to deal truthfully and faithfully with the little that has been entrusted in our hands.

Overcoming Intimidation

When his master handed everything concerning his house to Joseph, he did not give his wife to Joseph and Joseph was aware of the limits to his responsibilities. He was not responsible for his master's wife. How is this applicable to you? Assuming a boss at work has given you some special privileges, does that make you the boss?

Does that give you permission to use what belongs to your boss? Your special privileges have limits and you must adhere to them if you desire to maintain your position and special position in that company.

Let your light shine as a Christian

What has been made available to you are the only things you should be careful to manage and protect. Apart from that, any attempts to use or misuse company resources may be observed as an abuse of your position. When Jesus said, "He that is faithful with little is capable of being faithful with much" is a powerful and true statement (Luke 16.10). While Joseph used his humbled position of influence to only touch that which his master had entrusted him with, what are you doing with your position while in your era of dryness?

Have a right mindset at all times

Joseph's righh action was due essentially to his right mindset. What is your mindset? Having the wrong mindset is due to your social, cultural and mental conditioning. Having the wrong way of thinking is something that may limit you and cause you to do things that you will end up regretting later on in life.

Your mindset determines your destiny

Why is it that some people never make progress? It is partly due to their wrong mindset. If Joseph had the wrong training as a child and was exposed to immorality and immorality was the norm in his family and community, it would have been something else and his story might have been unpleasant to read.

You must be rooted and grounded in God

He would have seen that sexual move as an opportunity to practice his immorality. Jesus said, "If any man will come after me, let him deny himself and take up his cross and follow me "(Matthew 16.24).

To deny yourself means, you give God the first place in your life and count everything about yourself as secondary. That is not to say we should abandon our covenant responsibilities towards our families and loved ones.

Accept the call for a glorious life

It is simply a call to set our priorities right, to allow God to have the number one place in your life. All the cravings around you that seek to compete with kingdom responsibilities must be put under subjection.

When Joseph was faced with temptation to commit immorality with his master wife, he said,

Express when something is bothering you

"How can I do this great wickedness and sin against God" (Genesis 39.9)? His passion for God constrained him. You cannot love God and still be doing things contrary to His will. If you love Him, you will want to please Him at all costs. The power to give God the first place in your life has been granted you but will you activate it?

You have the mindset of the righteous

Due to his right upbringing, Joseph had developed a righteous mindset (synesis) and this mindset enabled him to overcome sexual temptation. One important thing to remember, as a Christian, is that you need to daily cultivate the right mindset. The word says we should be transformed by the renewing of our minds. Having the wrong mindset will land you into all sorts of troubles, thus in order to avoid regrets and heartbreaks, you need to do something about your current way of thinking.

Change your association to God fearing people

Associating with people who have the right mindset will enable you to develop your own. There is a saying that goes like this: "life is what you make it". That is absolutely right in the light of positive or negative patterns of thinking. You will find that those who fail miserably in life were people who had the wrong mindset.

Allow God's word to give you a new way of thinking

This principle also works not only in your social setting but it is also applicable to relationships. People with the wrong pattern of thinking find it difficult to develop good interpersonal relationships. The only way to change your negative way of thinking is having the right information; some people call it 'mental investment.' You are going to have to do some positive mental investment if you hope to cultivate and maintain the right mindset in every situation. Since your level of knowledge is the source of your current beliefs, having the correct information will enable you to form beliefs that will determine your mindset.

Your actions and words reveal your level of wisdom

The reason you do what you do is based on your beliefs hence before a right mindset, you need to evaluate your current beliefs. Where are the sources of your information or knowledge because these are the sources of your beliefs?

Cultivate the right way of thinking

What do you believe about yourself and where did you learn that information? Is it from God or from people? It is the quality of the information you feed on that determines what you believe. What do you believe about people in general? What do you believe about the opposite sex? What you believe determines your values and your values determine your mindset and your mindset determines your behaviour.

You should believe in God's testimony about you

Every significant person you see today came to become significant because of their mindset, which was based on the right information and that right information informed their decisions and choices in life. They are where they are not because of good luck, but it is based on what and whom they choose to believe.

Power of Belief

The law of believing is an important principle you need to cultivate. The only time an individual becomes connected to God, for whatever reason, is when they choose to believe the promise of God concerning a particular situation. The thing you need to know is that by believing, you have activated your faith in God and that simply means that you have invited the power of God in that situation.

Act on what you believe

The next thing you need to do is maintain speaking your beliefs and as you do, you are developing your belief system. As you work on your believing, it will become a conviction and that is when it will dawn on your spirit that you have got the answer to your situation. You must act as one who has already gotten the answer to that specific situation before it manifest; that sums up the key to receiving answers to your situation.

Key to Stepping into your Destiny

The key to stepping into your destiny and finally getting hold of what God has promised you in his word is accepting the promise of God for that specific situation as your answer. A person who believes in God has a continual open door in their life for God's visitation and impartation.

Keep working on your believing

The promise and the statements of facts you choose to believe is what will manifest in your life. By speaking what you believe, you are declaring before heaven and earth that, this is what you want to see happen in your life. When your believing has translated into faith, and then you have it made. Because confession precedes possession, you will have in your life what you continually say. (Mark 11.23).

Glorious things are spoken of you

Where you are at presently in life is a result of what you have been saying continuously. Secondly, what and who you have chosen to believe is what will manifest in your life. The difference between a successful individual and one who fails is based on what they each choose to believe. Your belief system is the force that determines your value system. What you value is what determines your mindset and your mindset determines your destiny.

Develop unbeatable believe

The only difference between a "somebody" and a "nobody" is that, "somebody" believed that they could remove any mountain on their path and because they believed in themselves, they became "unstoppable." On the contrary, a "nobody" believed that, one day they will become "nobody" and that is what they became. But a "somebody" believed that he or she will become "somebody significant" and nothing could stop each one of them from becoming what they believed they could become. While one used is "negative", the other used is "positive". This principle states that, "you are what you choose to be."

Know the God whom you serve personally

A typical illustration of the principle of believing is seen in the story of a young boy in the Bible called David. David believed that he could kill the greatest enemy of Israel at the time and that is exactly what he acted upon. By acting upon his believe he activated the power of God, facing Israel greatest and most notorious enemy he conquered him (1 Samuel 17.50, 2 Samuel 21.19). However, it all began with his decision to believe that it was possible.

Activate the universal law of success

No wonder Jesus said, all things are possible unto him that believes (Mark 9.23). The principle of believing states that if you believe that you are a failure, you will attract everything that is necessary and consistent with failure to ensure that you fail. If you believe that you are a success, you have activated a universal law which will attract all the resources in your life consistent with success and prosperity.

It is ok for you to succeed in life

The reason is, by believing you start talking what you believe because out of the abundance of the heart the mouth speaks and as you keep speaking it, you begin to create the necessary condition for the manifestation of what you have been confessing; thus the key to developing an unbeatable belief is repetition.

Identify a lying tongue

"Lies are like bats, as long as they are hidden in darkness, they elude everyone siliently and smoothly but when they are brought to daylight, they appear as the ugliest creatures on earth."

John H. Kekula

You are born for greatness

While Joseph overcame his master's wife sexual advances, he was falsely accused of sexual harassment. Without deliberation, Joseph was sentenced to prison. How many people do you think are in prison though they are innocent? Joseph found himself in prison because he chose to do the right thing. How many people are in prison all because they choose to do the right thing? How would you respond to a lie told against you?

You cannot be disadvantaged

In the case of Joseph, he was not given an opportunity to defend himself, however God was his defender. As long as Joseph was doing the right thing, God was with him. Being put in prison is the wrong place for a dream to come to pass but Joseph did not let go of his dreams in spite of his low location. While he was confined in a prison, he did not allow his present limitations to stop him from dreaming. He kept imagining the best.

Overcome a lying spirit

Let's examine a lying tongue and how it was used by Satan to take Joseph into prison. There is a principle concerning seeds and how when it is planted in the right soil and cultivated can quickly blossom. It will grow and become a mature tree, which begins to produce fruits. If it is a bad tree, the fruits produced will also be bad (Matt. 7.18).

Select your environment and create your atmosphere

A person who grew up in an environment that fostered a lying spirit will develop that to a point where lying becomes normal and automatic. Some parents sow the seed of lying into their children when children see their parents lying and cheating on each other. Those seeds are nurtured in children who begin to see it as something right and good.

Don't associate with liars

On the contrary, there are parents who are truthful but some of their children are liars and cheaters. The Bible says a lying tongue hates those it hurts (Proverbs 26.28). When a child is allowed to associate with liars, they begin to cultivate the spirit of lying because the law of association teaches or states that, those you associate with eventually influence you in their way of thinking and behaving and hence you become like them.

Therefore to avoid bad influence, do not allow your child to associate and spend quality time with liars.

Recognize a lying spirit

Probably if you understand the meaning of the word "law" you will begin to understand why you talk, act, and carry yourself the way you do. A law is a force that functions whenever you put it to work. When you associate with a lying spirit, it robs off on you and clings on you. You have exposed yourself to a lying spirit and it will want to turn you into a liar. By connecting with that spirit you have set the law of association in motion. The nature of a law is such that, when activated, it works to produce the desired result, negative or positive.

Learn how to activate a law

How do you activate a law? Simply by connecting yourself to a person who is already operating with a particular spirit, and when you do, you have set yourself up for an impartation from that person. Words are like water and they are seeds as well, when it is raining and you want to get wet, step into the rain and you will get yourself wet.

Be careful of what you are hearing

The words you are hearing are like rain, which is falling on those who are listening. The soil is your heart and when you listen to the wrong voice for very long, you are programming your spirit wrongly.

Words are not empty, they are full of instructions

Words that you hear can bring you down or build you up. So be careful who you associate with and listen carefully to what they are saying. What you are hearing and saying daily is what is responsible for creating your present hour reality.

Let the right seeds grow in your heart

When the seed of lies are sown, in order for the seed to grow and survive, it needs people who have grown in the spirit of lying to keep your own alive. There are some people who are fully grown and matured in a lying spirit. That is why some people just seem to get along so well because they have the same spirit.

Recognize and maximise the grace of God

When you read about Potiphar, his wife and Joseph, you will observe the result of an individual who was operating in a lying spirit. Since Joseph is symbolic of the graciousness of God, losing Joseph was like losing the grace of God in your life.

Losing Joseph is comparable to losing the ingredient that has been responsible for your success and prosperity. As long as Joseph was in Potiphar's house, the grace and favour of God was in that house and upon that house. Consequently losing Joseph was a loss of the help Potiphar had.

Conquer the lying tongue

One characteristic of the spirit of Jezebel is 'telling lies'; the mature Jezebel spirit has mastered the art of lying. When a Jezebel spirit tells a lie, it will appear as though he or she is telling the truth because she has matured a lying spirit. This account teaches and reveals how a Jezebel spirit operating in a lying spirit can be used to crush an individual. The following Bible verse reveals the power of a lie,

> With his mouth the godless destroys his neighbor, but through knowledge the righteous escape (Proverbs 11.9 New International Version).

Don't pollute your anointing

The next characteristic of Jezebel is that, it promotes godlessness and immoral behaviour. This negative character trait can be observed in Potiphar's wife demand for sex. You may be thinking why could a woman who is married demand sex from a slave boy living in their house?

Your destiny is preserved by associating with truth seekers

One thing you need to understand is the fact that she made herself available to be an instrument of destruction. The devil is in the business of aborting dreams and the day he found out about Joseph's dream and the hand of God upon his life, he was using every available means to abort the plans and purposes of God concerning Joseph's life.

Know the strategies and manoeuvres of your adversary

However, when she attempted and failed, she used another means and that is false accusation for sexual harassment. What does that teach us? It reveals that the devil is persistent. When the enemy comes one way and is defeated, he quickly finds another avenue to get his victims. In this case, a lying spirit in Jezebel presence in Joseph master's wife did the job. The next lesson to learn is that, as a significant person, you will come across liars who will tell lies about you and so be aware of that and stand firm on the truth.

Greatness attract troubles

The purpose of the lie told about you is not because you have done something wrong but because someone desires your position. Someone thinks you don't deserve the attention and position God has already given you or preparing to give you, hence they attempt to destroy your reputation.

Recognize and confine your enemy

You must always remember that the devil is the father of lies and like what took place in the beginning; the devil is attempting to steal your position from you (John 8. 44). Somebody is jealous of your position but in order to steal it from you, he first of all will need you to worship or do something that will give him the legal right to move and take your position.

One of the most effective weapon the devil has been using since the beginning of time is lies and the desire for power or self-gratification to steal the position of great men and women of God.

You have the power of discernment

The devil will make you think like you are nothing until you have done something he wants you to do. He did it to Adam (Genesis 3.4), He did it to Jesus (Matt. 4.1-11) and he is still doing it today. The devil will say you are not this significant person you thought you were until you have this and do this one thing. That one thing he is enticing you to do is going to cost you your destiny because that is the forbidden fruit. The Bible says, the wages of sin is death but the gift of God is eternal life through Jesus Christ our Lord. (Romans 3.23)

Attain to maturity of faith

There is one thing the devil is pushing you into doing and that will be the very thing that will destroy you and your destiny. I have discovered that, lack of self-identity is the major source of failure in life. If your Pastor has told you that you have a position with God and you don't do anything to understand and walk in the light of that revelation, the enemy will trick you into thinking you have no position.

Protect your position

By failing to operate from a position of authority you become a prey to the devil and those under his dominion. However knowing your true identity will make you very dangerous because, it makes you hard to handle. The devil will do anything to keep you from knowing who you are because the day you discover your true identity, you cannot compromise because you will not want to lose your authority with God. You will not tolerate any one who attempts to bring you to your knees.

As Joseph was tempted to bring himself lower and as a result compromise his destiny and position with God, so will you be tempted in your era of dryness.

Develop bullet proof identity

At every level of your era of dryness, you will be faced with the challenge of self-identity. Since your level of performance and achievement in life is directly related to your assessment of your worth, it is vital that you understand your true identity and begin to walk, act and talk like one who knows who they truly are. However, without knowledge of God's word, you cannot know who you are on a deeper and meaningful level.

Go after knowledge than anything else

The acquisition of godly knowledge then is fundamental to discovering your true self. Who are you to God? What has God said and done for you? As you read and learn what this book is teaching you, make it a reality by applying the principles.

Medidtate upon God's word

When knowledge is applied, it becomes knowledge that has been converted to produce a change. The way to convert knowledge, about who you are to become, is by believing what God has said about you and then confessing it with your mouth. If you desire to know what someone believes, listen to what they are saying to you; Jesus said, from out of the abundance of the heart the mouth speaks. (Matthew 7.12).

You are the born word of God

As a child of God, you are a new creation and you are the born word of God (1 Peter 1.23). That is why the Apostle Peter encourages every Christian to crave the word of God more than anything else in their life (1 Peter 2.2). You must value the word of God above anything else in your life if you desire to discover who you are and what has been made available to you.

You are an incredible person

This is how to grow your faith (Romans 10.17). This is how to attain to the maturity of faith, where you begin to use your faith to get anything you desire (Hebrews 5.13). You need to become skilful in the doctrine of righteousness.

Refuse to remain a baby

As long as you remain a baby Christian, as long as your faith is not developed, you will be under the elements of nature. You will be dominated by your five senses. Remaining a child (Greek: Nepio) will not make you any better than those who are in the world as far as your inheritance is concerned.

Your inheritance is awaiting your spiritual maturity

This fits in perfectly with the narration concerning Joseph's slavery and it helps us understand Joseph's slavery and troubles. It helps us to understand why God allowed Joseph to go through the persecutions.

Get out of your comfort zone

God was not interested in Joseph's comfort but was interested in bringing Joseph into his inheritance. You have to understand how God works in order to appreciate his way of doing things. God knew that Joseph will not develop in character if he remained in the comfort zone of his family and more importantly, his dream could not have been fulfilled because he was in the wrong location.

Refuse to let go of the word of God

From Joseph's life, we can learn that God wants us to develop character but character cannot be developed without persecutions and what brings persecution is when a person refuses to let go of the word of God (Matthew 13. 18-21).

God is developing longevity and durability in you

From that stand point then, if you are in a place in your life where you are experiencing tribulation and persecution, you should rejoice because it shows that you have not let go of the word of God or the dream God has given you. While that is easier said than done, that should be your attitude. Persecution is proof that you are a candidate for God's over all plans for humanity. Persecution is also an indication that character development is in progress and a person has refused to let go of their dreams.

Recognize your persecutor and resist him

As a result, Satan is using those around you and close to you to treat you badly in order to help you know what kind of person you truly are in the inside. If you do not know what you are made of, you will not see a need for change.

Welcome persecutions and troubles

But persecutions teach you about you and that in return teaches you to develop to become a better and stronger person in the inside. People who run away from difficult situations are prolonging their growth and development. On the other hand, if you desire to step into your destiny, you have to see every obstacle as a stepping-stone into the bright future God has in store for you.

Maturity brings you authority and power

When you see trials as opportunities, you are now beginning to understand the workings of God in your life. One important truth that you should always know is that, as a child of God, you have to grow into maturity because without it, you will not be given kingdom responsibilities.

Be honest about your spiritual status

But the way to grow into spiritual manhood may require that you begin to understand why you were placed in that situation. Is it to teach you obedience or is it because you have so much pride in your life and God has allowed those circumstances in your life in order to purify you from the spirit of pride?

Develop emotional toughness

For some, they get easily offended but God wants you to be so emotionally strong that offence will not have a way in your life. If you are an individual who gets their feelings hurt so easily, you can be sure that, you have not yet grown to overcome your flesh. What does God do in order to deliver you from the hurts that come from your five senses?

The people in your life are sent to reveal your level of maturity

He allows people to come into your life who are hurting you and as result, you will become aware of how fragile you are and if you are wise, you will run to God for help concerning your hurt feelings so that He can enable you to graduate to a higher level of spiritual and emotional strength.

Embrace spiritual maturity

People who get their feelings hurt too easily are still babes in Christ. You must grow to a point where you are not affected by how the devil is using people to talk about you. Stop asking the wrong questions, stop focusing on the wrong things in your life and start putting away childish things and begin on a journey of growing and maturing your character.

Your appointed time shall come

Only keep me in mind when it goes well with you, and please do me a kindness by mentioning me to Pharaoh and get me out of this house.

(Genesis 40:14 New American Standard Bible)

A man's gift makes a room for him

The chief butler did not remember Joseph because, it was not yet the appointed time, but when the fullness of time came, God reminded him, and Joseph was released and instantly promoted to Prime Minister of the whole of the Egyptian Empire.

Embrace your time of preparation

As we read in Galatians 4.1, the father has set an appointment time to give inheritance to his sons. This point is clearly revealed in Joseph's life. God gave Joseph a great dream but Joseph was not yet developed to handle the heavy responsibilities God wanted to release to him. God knew that Joseph needed to develop his character before he was released to fulfil his purpose. From this narrative, we can see that God will give you a dream or vision about the awesome future he has for you and then step back to prepare you for it.

God is grooming you for the throne

All those times Joseph was persecuted, God used those opportunities to prepare him for his destiny. The bigger the dreams you have been given the bigger the preparation you need to under go in order to see fulfilment of your dream. It is also true that, the bigger the building, the bigger and deeper the foundation has to be in order to sustain the building in times of storms.

Never rush in life

These are timeless truths, which are clearly observed in the lives of significant persons in every generation. But more importantly, God knows the conditions and the circumstances you need in your life to enable your preparation. God also knows exactly when you will be ready for that task. While many rush ahead of God, God on the other hand knew how to keep Joseph from not rushing ahead of him.

Recognize the hand of God and be grateful

The hand of God can be recognized in Joseph's life; he was confined in the pit and then he was placed in an Egyptian's house and finally, he was confined in the King's prison. As far as God was concerned, Joseph was in the right place, though it was certainly uncomfortable but God knew that at that time in Joseph's life that is the place he needed to be for preparation purposes.

Your present location is subject to change

There is a saying that accurately describes Joseph's situation, "where you are cannot define who you are, because who you are can only be defined by your creator". Joseph was in prison but the prison could not define who he was because he knew who he was. The knowledge of who you are will pilot you in your destiny. If you know who you are, it does not matter where you are presently. The truth of your situation is that, God has placed you strategically in a location where he wants to teach you certain important lessons that are directly related to your destination so that when you get to your destination you will know why you arrived and know exactly what to do.

You are becoming a wise and experienced person

When you finally get to your destination, you will begin to appreciate your journey because of the wisdom you have acquired. From a natural standpoint, being placed in a prison is unpleasant and you feel like things are only getting worse. As far as God is concerned you are on track, you are in the right place. God knows that your present location cannot define your true identity; it can only help to refine your current identity.

Use your words to create your future

The devil is the one responsible for many of your current troubles and ignorance is one of the deadliest weapons of the enemy. He creates those circumstances in order to see what you are going to do with those circumstances; the enemy's ultimate intention is to use you to destroy your future and destiny.

Put the enemy where he belongs

How does he succeed? By setting up circumstances in your life and then when you begin to see those circumstances in your life as your final reality, you begin to speak them. When you begin to speak what you see, you have unknowingly entered into an agreement (a covenant) with the devil.

Refuse to speak negatively about your life

As a result the devil keeps using your own negative confessions and pronouncements about yourself to poison your life and your destiny. The Bible makes it clear that death and life are in the power of the tongue and those who love it shall eat the fruit of it (Proverbs 18.21).It also says,

> "A fool's mouth is his destruction and his lips are a snare to his soul"
> (Proverbs 18.7 New International Version).

Speak life and not death

What you are saying is programming your spirit either for good or for evil. It is necessary to be aware of the fact that, in your time of dryness you will face the obstacle of your tongue attempting to sway you in the negative territory. What you do in your time of dryness with your tongue will determine how long you remain in that condition.

Recognize signs of your maturity

It is vitally important that you are aware of the power of your words because your words are an indication of your maturity or lack of maturity. Instead of using our words to ruin our lives and future, we should use it instead to shape our future by speaking the word of God at all times. Christian maturity according to Pastor Chris Ayakhilome (PHD) "is measured by the words you speak[6]".

You need to be relentless and highly persistent

It is very easy to speak what you see and have experienced, however, it takes men and women of significance to speak into being what they want to see instead of what they see or feel. Your ability to receive your inheritance is tied to your decision to speak life in your situation and not give up until you see a manifestation of those things you want manifested in your life. Speak life to every unpleasant situation in your life and watch the situation line up eventually to your confession.

Ezekiel 37.1-9 9 (New International Version)

> Then he said to me, "Prophesy to these bones and say to them, 'Dry bones, hear the word of the LORD! This is what the Sovereign LORD says to these bones: I will make breath enter you, and you will come to life. I will attach tendons to you and make flesh come upon you and cover you with skin; I will put breath in you, and you will come to life. Then you will know that I am the LORD.'"

> So I prophesied as I was commanded. And as I was prophesying, there was a noise, a rattling sound, and the bones came together, bone to bone. I looked, and tendons and flesh appeared on them and skin covered them, but there was no breath in them.

> Then he said to me, "Prophesy to the breath; prophesy, son of man, and say to it, 'this is what the Sovereign LORD says: Come, breath, from the four winds and breathe into these slain, that they may live. So I prophesied as he commanded me, and breath entered them; they came to life and stood up on their feet – a vast army.

Abraham was called "Abram" and God changed his name to reflect his destiny. The name "Abraham" means father of many nations. He kept calling himself a "father of many nations" though he did not have a child. That is exactly what you should do. You should call yourself what God has called you in his word everyday.

Your time of promotion is coming

So Pharaoh said to Joseph, "Since God has informed you of all this, there is no one as discerning and wise as you are. You shall be over my house, and according to your command all my people shall do homage; only in the throne I will be greater than you." (Gen. 41:39-50 New International Version)

Walk in the spirit everyday

When the father saw that Joseph had passed all the tests and had developed his character, he was ready to be released in his destiny. When destiny calls, will you answer? You have to be alert and discern the times to recognize your time when it comes. Your time will come but you will have to be ready by being yielded to the Holy Spirit.

Lack of maturity is what causes people to miss their time of visitation. The cause of lack of maturity is the lack of being yielded to the leading of the Holy Ghost. When you yield to the Holy Ghost, you grow really rapidly and begin to see the wisdom of God manifesting and functioning in your life.

Speak only the word of God at all times

The wisdom of God was manifested when Joseph opened his mouth because he had yielded to God and had matured as a result of his life experiences. Always remember that wisdom from experience is of lasting value and of great advantage. Hence, because he had yielded, the anointing took over immediately when Joseph opened his mouth to speak. When you are completely filled with the Holy Ghost, he speaks through you. (Ephesians 5.18)

Your time is coming, be ready for it

Pharaoh said to Joseph, "See, I have set you over all the land of Egypt (Genesis 41.41).

Partner with God to change the world

At the most crucial time of his life, the wisdom of God spoke through Joseph and the wisdom of God changed his status over night from a prisoner to a prime minister of the most powerful empire on the planet earth at that time. This narration shows us that God can change anything because he owns everything both the heavens and the earth and everything that dwell in them. But he needs a person to partner with him in carrying out his plans and purposes for the people of the earth.

God is the source of all power

Because he is the owner, he is more than able to give you anything you need to fulfil your destiny. (Psalms 24.1) It also proves that, God causes all things to work together for good for them that love Him and to them that are "The called" according to his purpose (Romans 8.28).

Wait for your appointed time

As long as you are yielded to the leading of the Spirit of God, everything you need to fulfil your purpose will come to you at the appointed time (Galatians 4.4, Romans 8.14).

Let hearing and obeying God be your primary goal in life

So the best thing you should do for yourself and God is to wait patiently on him to prepare you for your destiny and that is how you will overcome the era of dryness and reach your destiny (Ecclesiastes 3.11).

> For wisdom is better than jewels;
>> And all desirable things cannot compare with her.
> "I, wisdom, dwell with prudence, and I find knowledge and discretion.
>> "The fear of the LORD is to hate evil;
> Pride and arrogance and the evil way and the perverted mouth, I hate.
>> "Counsel is mine and sound wisdom;
> I am understanding, power is mine.
>> "By me kings reign, and rulers decree justice.
> "By me princes rule, and nobles,
>> All who judge rightly.
> "I love those who love me . . . ." (Proverbs 8.11-17)

FEAR

For God has not given us a spirit of fear, but of power and of love and of a sound mind (2 Timothy 1.7 (King James Version).

*I*n our final chapter, we are going to analyse the spirit of fear and why it is important to be aware of the assignment of fear as a major paralysing obstacle to stopping the significant person from fulfilling their dreams. If fear is allowed to have its way in your life, it will determine the course of your destiny.

Pull the plug on fear

In the same way when you decide to build your faith by hearing faith based teachings, you will grow your faith so strong that you can use it to get into your destiny no matter the challenges that come your way. In the same also fear can be developed to produce negative outcomes.

In this chapter we are going to find out the origin of fear and how the fountain of fear was dried up from your spirit when you got born again. We are going to look at how the spirit of fear came among the human race and why the spirit of fear til this day is the most destructive force on the planet. Finally, you will learn to develop the love of God so powerfully that it flushes out fear from your life. If fear is the most destructive force on the planet earth, you can be assured that love is the most constructive force on the planet.

Love conquers all

The importance of developing your love walk cannot be underestimated because perfected love, fully grown and mature love cast out or flushes out fear from your spirit and your soul (1 John 4.18 New International Version). In the same way love can be developed, that is the same way fear can also be developed to control your life.

You have the nature of the Father

The word says God is love and the source of truth (1 John 4.8) and hence Satan who is the resistor of God is the complete opposite of God. Since God is love, it is also true that Satan is hate and the father of lies. Lying is the very essence of the devil in the same way truth is the very essence of God. The more you practice walking in love on purpose, the more you develop the love of God in you.

> "The love of God is shared abroad in our hearts by the Holy Ghost" (Romans 4.28 New International Version).

Pay no attention to false evidence

Kenneth Copeland once said, "Fear is false evidence appearing real (FEAR)[7]." It is vital at the onset to note that, the opposite of faith is fear. Faith is the mode by which God operates. Fear is also the mode by which Satan operates. In other words, God does nothing without faith in the same way Satan does nothing without an element of fear.

Activate your faith in God

The same way faith, when activated, can work to produce the desired results so also fear when activated can function to produce a negative outcome. The Bible shows us how faith is acquired in (Romans 10.17); it says faith comes by hearing and hearing by God's word. How do you grow or increase your faith? It is by hearing God's word consistently and acting on what you hear. Since faith is the opposite of fear, fear also comes by hearing and hearing the lies of Satan.

Two kingdoms are in conflict

The words or voice of Satan is used to rule his kingdom and the words or voice of God is also used to rule and build his kingdom. Jesus said I will build my Church and the gates of hell shall not prevail against it (Matthew 16.18). Every time you listen to the word and act on what you hear, you are giving Jesus an opportunity to build you up.

Access Points of Fear

There are many avenues by which fear can enter your spirit, which are the media, newspapers and the words of close associates and the internet. It is worth noting also that God's representatives are also proclaiming the good news, which is capable of building faith and making a person wise.

Ignorance is Satan's weapon

The devil knows that, he can't do anything to you if you are walking by faith and building your faith. He knows that while faith connects you to God, fear connects you to Satan. Kenneth Copeland in his teaching on the "The Love Factor" said the following: "God can do nothing for you apart from faith as much as the devil can do nothing to you apart from fear"[8].

Acquire wisdom and understanding

This is vital because when you know this truth and apply it consistently, the devil's work ceases because you disconnect from him completely. That is the reason the Bible says, "Without faith, it is impossible to please God, he that comes to God must believe that He exists and that He is a rewarder of those who diligently seek Him" (Hebrews 11.6 New International Version). When you connect with God through faith, He works to perform everything He has promised in His words concerning you.

Never ever doubt God's word concerning you

The devil's work ceases in your world because you have chosen to be in agreement with God instead of the devil. Fear on the other hand makes you stand in agreement with the devil and when you do he is enabled, and more importantly you have empowered the devil to work in your life to destroy you. Since fear has the ability to destroy, whenever you activate it is crucial that you do not give a legal right or licence to Satan in your life.

Don't give a place to fear in your life

The word "fear" can be broken down to doubt and unbelief, yet faith can be described as a switch in your room. As long as the switch is off, there is no light in your room. The only way you can drive out light is by putting the switch off in your room. Faith can be compared to the switch and the light is the activation of your faith. The way you activate your faith is by acting on the words of God.

Clean out all garbage of fear from your house

Faith has to be understood because, it was through faith that God created everything you see and touch. It is through the spiritual force of faith that God created everything and they are activated and sustained by faith through the word of God. God's intention for you is to understand the way he functions and begin to imitate him as well (Ephesians 5.1).

Fear has lost its hold on you

Since the devil does exactly the opposite of what God does, it is vital to know how God operates. God uses faith to create, the devil uses fear, which is a counterfeit of faith to steal, kill and destroy. (John 10.10). Whatever God does, the devil does the opposite. While God is the creator, the devil is the destroyer. The devil is not a creator, he is not in God's class, neither is he in the human class; he is essentially in the angelic class with all its limitations.

ORIGIN OF FEAR

You have been declared free from fear

In order to establish the origin of fear, it is useful to read the book of Genesis to see how fear entered the human race. When you read the creation narrative, you will know that God created everything and it was very good.

The point of all failure is fear

There was nothing crooked or evil in everything God created (Genesis 1.31). God saw that all He had made and behold, it was very good. But when you read further, you will see that, God gave instructions to Adam about the tree of the knowledge of good and evil which he commanded him not to eat, because eating it would cause him to be disconnected from God (spiritual death). The account reads as follows: "but you must not eat from the tree of the knowledge of good and evil, for when you eat of it you will surely die.", (Genesis 2.17 New International Version).

God commands and instructions are for our protection

When God gave instructions on the danger of eating the fruit of the knowledge of good and evil and the bitter consequences, it was not because God was withholding something good from them. God was commanding them not to eat for their protection and preservation.

Choose the way of life

The instructions of the Lord are not meant to stop us from enjoying the good things in life. You need to understand that God is life and he knows what Adam and Eve needed but he also knew what would disconnect Adam and Eve from him and he also told them the dangers so that they could choose wisely (2 Timothy 3.15). When you read the account in (Genesis 3.1-10), you will discover that they chose to obey the serpent over the God who created them. By choosing to obey an alien creature through the serpent, they disobeyed God and were separated from God, thus they were now connected to Satan who is the death angel. The nature of Satan was imparted in them and they begin to function exactly like Satan.

Don't listen to Satan lies and deceptions

This narrative shows the origin of fear and the avenue by which fear was introduced in the human race. They heard the sound of the Lord God walking in the garden in the cool of the day, and the man and his wife hid themselves from the presence of the Lord among the trees of the garden.

Man began to function in fear

Then the Lord God called to the man, and said to him "Where are you?" He said, "I heard the sound of you in the garden and I was afraid because I was naked, so I hid myself" (Genesis 3.10). This narrative shows the beginning and the source of fear. When Adam and Eve disobeyed God, the result was a complete disconnection from God. Since no human is sovereign, a disconnection from God was automatically a connection to the death angel.

Man became a victim of his environment

The serpent is typified in the Bible as the devil; hence in the garden the devil used a snake to deceive Eve in eating the forbidding fruit and gave some to her husband which resulted in spiritual death. Since the devil is the spirit of fear and can only function by fear, a connection to him meant that, Adam and Eve were now functioning exactly as the devil functions. Since Adam and Eve were connected to God through faith, a disconnection from God who functions by faith resulted in a connection to Satan who functions by fear.

The Law of Reciprocity

Kenneth Copeland points out in his teachings on the freedom from fear, that the law of reciprocity was activated during the fall. Kenneth Copeland also observed based on what the Lord said to him that there is a Bible law of reciprocal actions. He goes on to give an illustration describing how this law functions in the positive and the negative to produce desired output.

Take your stand against fear

The reciprocal of the south is the north. When you begin a journey southward, you will keep going south until you decide to turn back and when you do, you have just begun a journey north. I don't care how far you have travelled south as soon as you turn and decide to go back you are headed north. This also applies to faith and fear. As south is the exact opposite of north, so also faith is the exact opposite of fear and they work to produce the exact opposite results.

The devil hates God's creation

Now, when the devil saw Adam and Eve and saw the likeness of God in them, he came and succeeded in deceiving them into coming out of the covering of God into the devil's territory. When they disconnected from God and connected to Satan, they began to function like him. They were no longer operating in God's atmosphere and protection. The devil became their Lord and master.

Death began regning in the human race

The faith through which they were connected to God and functioned like God became fear. Hence fear is twisted faith. What was divine health became sickness. What was prosperity became poverty. What was peace became turmoil, discouragement and despondency and what was love became hate. According to Kenneth Copeland," this is the law of reciprocal and it was activated by the disobedience of Adam and Eve. So fear is simply, your faith in the ability of a snake attempting to harm you"[9].

Fear is the source of death

When you understand that whatever the devil does and says is a complete opposite of what God would say, you begin to counter anything and everything the devil say with the law of reciprocal. For example, when the devil says, "You are a disaster" you understand that, whatever the devil has said is a reciprocal of what God would say.

Refuse to yield to fear filled words

You are a disaster should be countered with "I am a success, a master and a joy and an expression of the glory of God. In everything I do, I am expressing the glory of God because I am essentially born to show forth the glory of God. In my walking and talking, I am showing forth his glory because I am the glory of God. In fact I am not a disaster because God does not create disasters".

Anyone who says that "You are crazy, mad, stupid, and dumb and an idiot and your family know that, you are foolish and you have no future" are speaking lies from the pit of hell.

All insecurities come from fear

You have a responsibility not to believe those lies from hell but to reject them immediately. Many who believe what they hear from the devil and believe him live mediocre lives. When he says you are a loser, tell him you are a winner and more than a conqueror in Christ Jesus our Lord. When he says you are a failure, say I am a success and I know that God does not create failures.

Fear is a destructive force

Whenever you feel discouraged or down, don't say what you feel. Always remember that you are the one in charge and you are the one with the power to determine how you feel. Learn to turn every weakness to strength with the word of God. The Bible says, "Let the weak say I am strong and the let the poor say I am rich (Joel 3.10 King James Bible)". You have the law of the spirit of life at your disposal and God expects you to use it. The Lord expects you to use the whole armour of God (Ephesians 6.9).

Your faith filled words dominates the realm of the senses

Instead of allowing the devil to make you feel fear; you need to put him to flight by your faith filled words (2 Timothy 1.7). Your angels are at your disposal but you need to learn to dispatch them to act on your behalf (Hebrews 2.16). God expects the double-edged sword to be in your mouth at all times. (Psalms 149.6)

Locating your Source

The importance of knowing your origin is an absolute necessity to overcoming the spirit of fear. One of the advantages is that, it helps you appreciate yourself and it also helps you to take your rightful place and inheritance in Christ Jesus. When you put things in their proper perspective, it enables you also to understand that you are superior to Satan and have no business being connected to him through the spiritual force of fear.

You are a wonder

According to Dr. Myles Munroe, "when God made trees and plantations, he spoke to the earth to produce it. The source of trees and vegetations is the soil or the ground, hence the essence of plants and vegetations are hundred percent dirts."[10] More importantly, the source from which trees and plants came is the soil; as a result, their continual existence is dependent on their connection with the soil. It demonstrates that, the source of a thing determines the kind of life it experiences.

You are a super star

The second example is the life of a fish. When God wanted fish, he spoke to the waters. The waters produced all sorts of living creatures at God's command. When a fish is taken out of the water, it dies because it has been disconnected from its source. Since God commanded the waters to bring forth living creatures, the sustenance and preserver of living creatures is their source. This principle reveals that, you are sustained, upheld and preserved by your source.

You have the power to achieve any goal in your life

The next example is the fowl of the air. The fulfilment and satisfaction only comes to birds when they flip and fly in the sky. God created them with the ability to fly and the sky is their domain.

When you deprive birds of the ability to fly, you have just destroyed their primary purpose of existence.

Your source gives your life a meaning

God also applied the same principle when he created man. When God created all other creatures, he never spoke to himself; he always spoke to the ground, seas, and sky. However, when it came to the creation of man, he spoke to himself. This is the greatest act God ever did because it reveals that, the source from which man came is God. Only human beings were created in God's class not even angels. Hence, to function properly, man needs to be connected to God and remain in his presence. It is through faith in Christ that brings the connection between man and God.

---

[10] Myles Munroe, Releasing Your Potential, (Destiny image publishers: USA, 2002), 73, 88

Man's Position

We thank God that when Jesus came, he overcame the devil and stripped him of all his authority and handed back the dominion mandate to man. After his resurrection, Jesus made this profound declaration: "All authority in heaven and on earth has been given unto me, therefore go into the entire world and preach the gospel to every creature, baptizing them in the name of the Father, Son and the Holy Spirit"(Matthew 28.18 New International Version).

In this verse Jesus Christ handed down all authority in heaven and on earth to his disciples and to every believer who receives the message of the kingdom. The Son of God was manifested that he might destroy the works of the devil (1John 3.8 New International Version).

You now have the power to determine your destiny

The devil is no longer a factor

It is important to remember that one of the greatest arsenals in the devil's weaponry is fear. While Satan was completely paralyzed and left powerless, the only thing he uses now is fear to stop, harass and destroy people lives because that is the only major weapon he has got in his kingdom.

Satan rules the kingdom of darkness

The devil uses fear to control, dominate and to terrorise his victims. Why do you think good news does not sell as much as bad news? It is because Satan dominates the system of this world and hence the words of the devil seem to prevail in every sphere of society where the Gospel of the good news is not preached.

The New Creation

You are superior to Satan

As we read the book of Hebrews, we will see exactly what God said about the new creation that came into being as a result of Jesus' obedience to death.

The writer of Hebrews states:

> "For to which of the angels did he ever say, you are my Son, today I have begotten you, and again, I will be a Father to him and he shall be a Son to me. And when He again brings the first born into the world, He says and let all the angels of God worship him." Hebrews 1.5-6 (English

Standard Version). In the book of Hebrews, God makes the most profound declaration about his first born Son.

It goes as follows: But of his Son he says,

> "Your throne oh God is forever and Ever. And righteous sceptre is the sceptre of your kingdom. You loved righteousness and hated lawlessness. Therefore God, Your God has anointed you with the oil of gladness above your companions. And you, Lord, in the beginning laid the foundation of the earth and the heavens are the works of your hands; they will perish but you remain and they will become old like a garment and like a mantle you will roll them up; like a garment they will also be changed. But you are the same and your years will not come to an end." (Hebrews 1.8-12 English Standard Version)

You have authority and tremendous power

These verses we have just read are among the greatest scriptures because it reveals the words used to bring the head of the new creation into the world Jesus Christ. Since we are joint heir with Jesus, those same declarations apply to us. When you received Christ, you became a new creation and God used those words to create you.

Romans 8.17

And if children, then heirs – heirs of God and fellow heirs with Christ, provided we suffer with him in order that we may also be glorified with him (English standard version).

You are in God's class

As those who have been born again, we have a high position with God (2 Corinthians 5.17). The devil is hoping that you will not know or become aware of who you are in Christ. The devil knows that when you find out your identity in Christ, you will begin to rise above anything that he attempts to put on you unlawfully. Not even the angels have a privileged position as you do because you are a Son of God as much as Jesus is a Son of God.

God loves you as much as he love Jesus

Jesus is the first born amongst many brethren. (Romans 8.29) and the authority God conferred on Christ when He raised him from the dead is the same authority

Jesus conferred unto us when we got born again. As a new creation that has been re-created in the image of him who created you, you have the advantage over angels and as far as Satan is concerned, you are superior to him and he has no position unless you gave it to him through your negative confessions (Ephesians 4.24).

You are a god as far as Satan is concerned

Where does that place fear? Where does that place failure or poverty? As a son of the most-high God, you have authority and power in your mouth and you can use it to create, maintain the structure and the administration of your world. It does not matter the confusion you see around you, it does not matter what people are saying about you and it does not even matter what Satan is saying because what matters most is what God has said about you.

You were born a champion

You need to lock yourself up to God and everything he has said about you and begin to say it until you become it. (2 Timothy 2.15) Circumstances will come and go but God's word remains forever and it has the divine potency to change anything you desire to change that has not yet aligned itself or is inconsistent with the life of the new creation. (Hebrews 4.12).

You are the inheritor of the Abraham blessing

Your job is your labour of faith which, demands speaking those things that be not as though they were (Romans 4.12). Your job is to resist anything that God has not given you and use the sword of the spirit to cut down anything God has not planted your life (Hebrews 4.12).

The devil obeys your voice

The scripture says, "God has not given us the spirit of fear but of power, love and of a sound mind" (2Timothy 1.7). The word also makes it clear that, when you submit yourself to God and resist the devil, he will flee from you (James 4.7).

The devil is subject to you

Now that you know who you truly are in relation to God, it should make you more confident in facing the challenges that you have been facing due to what you did not know. On the contrary because of what you know now, the devil cannot use fear to control your destiny. You can now use your faith to control your destiny.

You must use your words to create and maintain your world

Kenneth Copeland said, "When the enemy aims at a life, he uses fear because this is the most effective weapon he has been using since the beginning of the creation of man."[10] He used fear of loss in the garden to overcome Adam and Eve and has learned from experience that, there are other forms of fear that are equally effective in stopping and disconnecting an individual from fulfilling their destiny.

You are a master of your destiny

Before we get into this important discussion, let us summarise or emphasize the superiority of the new creation of God over Satan and all his works of darkness. First of all, it is important to note that, man was created in the image and likeness of God. Man was the god of this earth. He had total dominion mandate and absolute power over the affairs of the earth.

Man is God's representative on earth

However man lost this authority to rule when they bowed to Satan, but Jesus came to destroy the devil and his works so that we can carry out our original dominion mandate (Hebrews 2.15). Jesus was the second Adam and he reclaimed everything the devil inherited from Adam and gave it back to all mankind who will accept his sacrifice. Now that Satan has lost his rights to Lord it over you, you have power to be all that God has placed in your heart to accomplish.

So it is written: "The first man Adam became a living being the last Adam, a life-giving spirit." (1 Corinthians 15.45)

You are now a giver of life

However since the devil has the right to present you with all sorts of fear, you need to be aware of his strategies and schemes of operation. So long as you are in this world, the five senses are the tools by which the devil will constantly use to present things to you because he is an outlaw and he is constantly working to make you see things his way instead of God's way. However, if he can get you to accept his offers, you have given him an open door to your life through the spiritual connector of fear.

You have power to dominate circumstances of life

It has been said by Kenneth Copeland that, "you cannot fight thoughts with thoughts but you can fight thoughts with words."[11] In other words you have the power to control your thoughts by your words. Your thoughts will listen to your words and they will follow your words.

Take on the shield of faith and be on the offensive

The devil is also aware of this principle and so he will do things in order to make you feel a certain way so that you begin to say what you feel. As you begin to say what you feel, you have given Satan the licence to bring to pass what you are saying because you are operating in the negative realm and the negative realm or the relam govern by the senses is Satan's domain. (Romans 8.2)

Satan has power in the realm common to the natural man

Your "feelings" if negative will always lie to you, that is why you need to go against what your negative emotions are telling to you. The voice of your spirit is your 'conscience', the voice of your soul is your 'reasoning' and the voice of your body is your 'feeling'.

Learn to subdue your senses

The devil can only have access to your life through your mouth and your five senses. However faith, which is the exact opposite of fear, is not found in the sense realm. In other words, faith transcends rationality, it does not make sense because it is above logic, that is why the word says, the just shall live by faith (Romans 1.12) and anything that does not proceed from faith is sin (Romans 3.21). Faith is not found in the soul and faith is not found in the flesh and the body. Faith is only found in your spirit. Faith is the response of the human spirit to God's word.

Dictate to your senses at all times

Walking by faith and speaking words of faith is the surest way to live like God. A person who walks by faith has rightly positioned themselves and aligned themselves with God and this in turn gives God the licence to move into their life to bring to pass whatever they have been saying and confessing daily. (Hebrews 3.1) Since the presence of fear is the absence of faith, you can easily begin to eliminate any forms of fear by filling your life with faith based resources.

You are now living in the realm of pure possibilities

When you are constantly filled with faith, the enemy cannot have access in your life because you have taken the first step in destroying the stronghold of fear in your life (2 Corinthians 10.4) On the other hand, if you are moved by how you feel, you are drifting into doubt and unbelief and this is toxic to your inner man because you have stopped walking by faith.

Guard your heart against fear and unbelief

By continually talking and confessing the word of God and listening to it daily, you are building your faith and programming your spirit for success. Keep speaking the word don't stop talking it! Welcome to the realm of pure possibilities!

ACKNOWLEDGEMENTS

This book would not have been made possible without the contribution from Dr. Myles Munroe. There are a number of other authors like Dr. Mike Murdock, Pastor Chris Ayakhilome (PHD), Pastor Tayo Ojo, Pastor Benny Hinn, Dr. Creflo Dollar and Arch-Bishop Nicholas Ducan-Williams and many others. These have influenced my thinking and have caused me to understand the reason I am here. The teachings of Kenneth Copeland have been a great source of discovery in my life as well. The Kenneth Copeland teaching on the 'Freedom from fear' has changed me completely, and I will be forever grateful to Kenneth Copeland for sticking to his calling no matter the obstacles that he has experienced.

When Dr. Samuel Author became my Pastor in 2002, my life took on a new meaning and your teachings Pastor Samuel are life transforming.

My Father, John Hailey Kekula is the one who helped me to believe that anything is possible. As one with a Master degree in Civil Engineering, his experience and special areas of knowledge has been of great advantage to me and to this book.

The last but not the least is my entire family and friends who have motivated me to keep writing because they were waiting for the time this book would be available to them and in book stores. I am very grateful to you all for your encouragement and support. A special thank goes to John H. Kekula, Rhonda Devonish, Sherphi Heric Antonio, Teniesha Duhaney, Lisa Tremlet who were the editors of this great book. Thanks a lot guys!

ENDNOTES

1   Dr Myles Munroe, Bahamas Faith Ministries International Fellowship, TBN, 2006

2   Pastor Benny hinn, Operating in the anointing, CD series, Benny Hinn Ministries 2005

3   Beyond the veil, entering into intimacy with God through prayer, Published by Renew books, from Gospel light, ventura, California, USA, pg 122, 1997)

4   ArchBishop Nicholas Duncan-Williams, Overseer of Christian Action Faith Ministries, prayer summit, Manchester 2007

5   Kenneth Copeland, "The Love Factor", CD Series, Kenneth Copeland Ministries, Fort Worth Texas

6   Pastor Chris Ayakhilome PHD, Christ Consciousness DVD Series, Believer's Love World President

7   Kenneth Copeland, Kenneth Copeland Ministries Fort Worth Texas 'Freedom From Fear, CD Series,

8   The Love Factor, CD Series, Kenneth Copeland Ministries Fort Worth Texas

9   Freedom From Fear Series, Kenneth Copeland Ministries, Fort Worth Texas

10 Kenneth Copeland, "The Love Factor" Kenneth Copeland Ministries, Fort Worth Texas

11 Releasing The Love Of God In You, Kenneth Copeland Ministries, Fort Worth Texas
    Nothing before the time but God's timing is the best was a quote I heard from Dezrene Pascall